STOP!...AND READ THIS BEFORE MAKING YOUR FIRST FILM

STOP!...AND READ THIS BEFORE MAKING YOUR FIRST FILM

ZOLTAN L DEAK

PILLANGO
PUBLISHING

CONTENTS

1 INTRODUCTION   1

2 INTRODUCTION to the 2nd EDITION   5

3 WHY AM I DOING THIS AND WHO IS IT FOR?   9

4 WHY MOST FIRST-TIME FILMMAKERS FAIL   13

5 WHAT TO DO, WAY BEFORE SHOOTING YOUR FILM?   24

6 CHOOSING THE RIGHT FILM TO MAKE   31

7 FINANCING YOUR FILM   37

8 FINDING PROFESSIONAL INVESTORS   44

9 FILM REBATES   54

10 I HAVE A SCRIPT AND THE MONEY!...NOW WHAT?   59

11 BUILDING YOUR TEAM   65

12 CHOOSING YOUR DIRECTOR   72

13 LOCATIONS   76

14 PRE-PRODUCTION   84

15 POST-PRODUCTION   88

16 BILLING BLOCKS AND CREDITS   94

17 SALES AGENTS — 98

18 DISTRIBUTORS — 102

19 UNDERSTANDING BUYOUT CONTRACTS — 106

20 DELIVERY REQUIREMENTS — 114

21 IN CONCLUSION — 120

BONUS CONTENT — 122

The Author — 123

CHAPTER 1

INTRODUCTION

My name is Zoltan Deak, and I'm a full-time film producer.

I decided to write this book because I have reached a point in my career where I feel confident enough to share advice, especially for those of you preparing to shoot your first feature film. I shot mine at the end of 2023 and sold it two years later. It was one of the hardest three years of my life. That experience inspired me to create this book. I hope to spare others from facing the same challenges and to prepare them for the monumental journey of producing a feature film.

Make no mistake, it will still be tough. With the right preparation and knowledge, however, you will have the tools to navigate the process with more confidence and less stress. This book will help you understand what to watch for so you are not caught off guard.

Producing your first feature film is both amazing and intimidating. I want to make it a little less overwhelming by sharing everything I have learned so far. With the right mindset and preparation, you can set yourself up for success, and reading this book is a strong place to begin.

I made the mistakes, so you do not have to.

Now, let me tell you a bit about myself.

I was born in Pécs, Hungary, where I currently live. When I was 12, my family moved to Australia, and I spent most of my formative years there. In 2015, I decided to return to Hungary permanently.

From a young age, I was captivated by film. I did not know which aspect fascinated me most, but from the time I was five or six, I knew I wanted to be part of it in some way. I still remember being mesmerized by our small black-and-white television in the 1970s. Programming was limited, so whenever a cartoon or film aired, it felt like an event.

When it came time to choose a career after finishing school in Australia, I found myself at a crossroads. I was unsure what opportunities were available, so I followed a different path. I studied accounting and worked in the field for about five or six years. Later, I joined my father's roofing business in property maintenance. Eventually, I became interested in computers, which led me to study hardware and software. That opened the door to a job at Silicon Graphics, a company that, at the time, was a leader in high-end graphics and supercomputers.

Working at Silicon Graphics was an incredible experience. The company developed cutting-edge hardware technology used in Toy Story, other early animated films, and the visual effects for The Lord of the Rings films. I loved the work, the people, and the opportunities to travel, from Bangkok to San Francisco to Silicon Valley. In 2003, the company filed for Chapter 11 bankruptcy, and I was laid off. It was devastating at the time, but looking back, it became a turning point.

Losing that job gave me the push I needed to pursue my passion for filmmaking. I started small, launching a business with my partner, installing plasma screens in shopfront windows, which was a novel idea at the time. Unfortunately, the venture failed due to my lack of business experience and the fact that we were simply too early to market. We lost a significant amount of money, including savings from my parents, and I had to start over.

To rebuild, I sold my flat and invested the proceeds in camera equipment. That was when my filmmaking journey truly began. I bought a camera, lighting gear, and a laptop, and I taught myself everything through trial and error. This was before online tutorials were widely available. I started with small projects, corporate videos, short films for sales meetings, and even wedding videos.

It was not enough to make a living, so I continued working part-time in my father's property maintenance business while dedicating every spare moment to filmmaking. Over time, I developed skills in editing, graphics, and design, adapting to new technologies as they emerged.

Eventually, I landed my first job on a feature film as a best boy in the lighting department. It was a 20-day shoot, and I loved every second of it, the camaraderie, the creative energy, and the excitement of being on set. That experience opened the door to more opportunities. I became friends with the gaffer, Mark, who brought me onto television commercials and other projects. When Mark left the industry, he gave me some of his lighting gear in exchange for helping him sell his larger equipment. That equipment allowed me to work as a gaffer on short films and features for the next five years, which proved to be an invaluable learning experience.

During those years, I witnessed firsthand how feature films are made and, at times, how they fall apart, whether in post-production or distribution. Unfortunately at least 50% failed before reaching the finish line. Despite the challenges, I fell in love with the collaborative nature of filmmaking and the magic of bringing stories to life.

In 2015, I returned to Hungary and set my sights on helping develop the film industry in my hometown of Pécs. Budapest, the capital, is one of the largest production hubs in Europe, and I wanted to bring some of that activity to our region. I began networking with local filmmakers and producers, and we started collaborating on projects.

We began with a television commercial and eventually moved on to a children's educational television series, which I directed and produced for four years, creating around 360 episodes. Later, my company built a virtual set for national weather forecast, integrating advanced green-screen and three-dimensional technology with weather software from The Weather Company in the United States.

After selling that company, I shifted my focus to strengthening the film industry in Pécs. In 2022, I partnered with a UK investor to build an audio post-production studio. The following year, with support from local investors, I shot an English-language feature film aimed at the U.S. market. Now, in 2026, I am working on multiple feature film projects.

My goal is to share everything I have learned to help you navigate your first feature film. From planning and production to selling your film, I want to equip you with the tools not only to survive the process but to emerge with a finished product you are proud of and ready to move on to your next major venture.

Let's get started!

CHAPTER 2

INTRODUCTION to the 2nd EDITION

Hello, and welcome to the second edition of this book.

If you've read the first edition, you might be wondering why I decided to update it. The simple answer is this: since publishing the first edition, a lot has happened and some of it fundamentally changed what I thought I already knew.

The biggest reason for this update is the film I referenced throughout the first edition.

At the time of writing, we believed the film was sold.

We received what is known as a deal memo. It came after months of discussions, negotiations back-and-forth with a distributor through our sales agent. Everyone involved believed it was a done deal. The money was not what we had originally hoped for, but it was reasonable. Most importantly, it meant I could repay the investors, pay the crew and actors what they were owed, and finally get the film out into the world so that everyone's credit would carry more weight than if the film remained on the shelf.

I would not have made back the money I invested, but that was something I had already accepted. At that stage, the priority was not profit. It was closure, fairness, and distribution. Sometimes in this business, you have to be realistic and grateful for what you can secure.

Then, three months later, after a long wait that included the Christmas period, the distributor decided not to proceed.

Just like that, the deal was gone.

By then, the first edition of this book had already been published. I could not afford to wait indefinitely for a final decision, and I did not have the time or resources to delay or rewrite the book while the situation remained unresolved. So the book went out into the world based on the information I had at the time.

This second edition exists because honesty matters.

The good news is that we eventually secured a sale with another distributor. Unfortunately, it was for considerably less money, which made things more difficult financially. Once again, however, the most important outcome was that the film was finally distributed. Just as importantly, the process taught me lessons I could not have learned any other way.

In this edition, I'm going to go deep into what actually happened.

I'll walk you through:

- Why the first deal collapsed
- How the second deal came together
- What changed between the two
- And what those changes meant financially, legally, and emotionally

Most importantly, I'm going to break down the contract in detail.

Because here's the truth:

Everything that happens at the end of a film's life is determined by decisions you make at the very beginning.

Contracts affect how money flows, who gets paid first, who has control, what deliverables are required, how credits are negotiated, and whether or not a deal can even close. These are things first-time filmmakers rarely think about until it's too late.

This edition also expands into areas that are constantly overlooked, yet regularly cause serious conflict:

- Deliverables: what distributors actually require, why missing one item can delay or kill a deal, and how E&O (Errors and Omissions) insurance fits into all of this
- Billing blocks and credits: the order of names on posters, IMDb listings, and on-screen credits, and why this becomes a serious issue once a film is sold
- Partnerships: how to structure them properly from day one, define responsibilities clearly, and avoid the all-too-common problem where one party does most of the work but everyone expects the same reward
- Sales agents and distributors: through direct conversations and interviews, we'll look at how they think, what they expect, and where misunderstandings usually arise

Many of these issues do not feel important when you are simply trying to get your film made. They become important the moment money, credit, and control enter the conversation. By then, emotions are high, relationships are strained, and mistakes are costly.

This second edition is not about theory. It is about lived experience, updated with the benefit of hindsight, failure, recovery, and real contracts signed under real pressure.

If the first edition was about helping you avoid losing everything while making your first film, this edition is about making sure that when your film does sell, you are prepared for what comes next.

Thank you for being here.

I hope this expanded edition helps you avoid some of the mistakes I had to learn the hard way.

Please enjoy.

CHAPTER 3

WHY AM I DOING THIS AND WHO IS IT FOR?

Why Am I Doing This?

One of the main reasons I'm doing this is to make sure that anyone starting on this journey has as much real-world information as possible and, ideally, avoids some of the mistakes I made.

And there were many.

The last five years of my life have been the hardest I've ever experienced. A large part of that difficulty came from making my first feature film and navigating everything that came with it. The mistakes I made were not just creative or technical. They were financial, legal, and strategic. Some cost money. Some cost time. Others took a serious toll on me mentally and emotionally.

Making a film can break you if you are not prepared for what is coming.

I learned a tremendous amount through that process, but it came at a very high price. Financially, it put me under pressure for years.

Emotionally and mentally, it tested me in ways I was not ready for at the time. There were moments of doubt, exhaustion, frustration, and stress that I would not wish on anyone, especially someone making their first film without fully understanding what they are truly stepping into.

This book exists because I do not believe others should have to learn these lessons the hard way.

Yes, you should absolutely do your own research. Yes, you should read as many books as you can. But what is often missing from most filmmaking advice is honesty about risk, responsibility, power dynamics, money, contracts, and the emotional weight that comes with carrying a project from idea to distribution.

My goal is simple: if you are going to do this, you should go in with your eyes open.

Who Is This For?

If you are reading this, I am assuming you have already worked in the film industry in some capacity for a while. Maybe you have made a short film or two. Maybe you have worked in different departments. Maybe you have assisted, coordinated, or even produced something already. You are likely at the point where you are thinking seriously about making your first feature film.

Let me be very clear: there are countless things to consider. Never rush into it.

Most films take years to get made, two, three, five, sometimes even ten years from concept to completion. My first feature film took around three years from the initial idea to a finished product. That was not because we were slow or unmotivated. Most of that time was spent raising money, assembling the right team, identifying potential buyers, negotiating deals, and managing countless details that most people never see. This stage is called development, and it is where many projects quietly die.

So my advice is simple: take your time.

There is absolutely no reason to rush into making a feature film until you are confident that everything is in place. In later chapters, I will go into detail about what "having your ducks in a row" actually means, because it is far more than just having a script and a camera. I am also assuming that you have taken some courses, maybe gone to film school, or at least gained hands-on experience. If you have not, my strongest advice is this: do not start with a feature film.

Start with a short film or films.

Gather your friends, put together a small project, and make mistakes on something that will not financially or legally ruin you. Short films are far less risky, but they will teach you the fundamentals: working with crew, managing actors, solving problems under pressure, and finishing what you start.

If you are moving forward with your first feature film, start small. Do not jump straight into a $5 million production, even if you have made short films or worked on set. Most filmmakers begin with a low-budget feature, often in the $50,000 to $100,000 range, with an unknown cast and a contained concept. As you gain experience, you can scale up.

Remember this: the larger the budget, the larger the responsibility and the greater the consequences when something goes wrong.

Experience matters.

Another important piece of advice is to consider teaming up with an experienced producer. Working alongside someone who has already made one, two, or three films can be invaluable. You will learn more by collaborating with someone experienced than by trying to carry the entire burden yourself. It is one of the safest ways to move forward without taking on risks you are not ready to handle yet.

And finally, this book is not only for producers.

Writers, especially screenwriters, should read this book as well.

I regularly receive messages from writers asking whether their script is "good enough" to get made or whether I would take it on as a producer. What many writers do not fully understand is the level of responsibility, risk, time, and work required to turn a script into a finished, distributed film. A great script is only the beginning. The journey from page to screen is long, complex, and filled with obstacles that have nothing to do with writing.

Understanding what it actually takes to get a film made will make you a better collaborator, a more realistic creative partner, and ultimately increase your chances of seeing your work produced.

It is for people who are ready to take their next step in filmmaking but want to do so wisely, strategically, and with a clear understanding of the risks involved. Anyone can read this book and learn something, but the core message is this:

Only take on projects you are truly prepared to carry.

Filmmaking is exciting, creative, and deeply rewarding, but when it goes wrong, the consequences can be severe. Financial debt, damaged reputations, broken relationships, and even legal trouble are very real possibilities.

Take your time.

Plan carefully.

And let me guide you through the process so you can learn from my mistakes!

CHAPTER 4

WHY MOST FIRST-TIME FILMMAKERS FAIL

One of the greatest challenges faced by first-time filmmakers is not the actual production of their film. It is what happens after it is made. If I could give you a single piece of advice, the most important takeaway from this book would be this: learn the business of filmmaking before you start making a film.

I have seen it happen countless times, months, even years, of hard work completely derailed because filmmakers did not anticipate the obstacles waiting for them after the cameras stopped rolling. I have watched talented individuals spend all their resources making a feature film, only to find that once it was finished, they could not sell it. Worse still, they lost important documentation, had disputes with cast members, or ran into logistical nightmares that made distribution impossible. These challenges can leave filmmakers demoralized, financially devastated, and creatively stifled for years.

This chapter is about helping you avoid those pitfalls. If you take the time to learn how the film market works, you will not only save yourself money but also countless hours of frustration.

The Hardest Part of Filmmaking: Selling the Film

Many first-time filmmakers think that writing, directing, and producing a film will be the hardest parts of the process. They imagine that once their masterpiece is finished, everything will fall into place. Distributors will rush to acquire the film. Accolades and revenue will pour in. Unfortunately, that is rarely the case.

Selling your film and making your money back is by far the hardest part of filmmaking. In fact, most first-time producers do not seriously consider distribution until it is too late. They are so focused on their script and production that they fail to consider how their film will be positioned in the marketplace. They assume the brilliance of their story will carry it through.

The Producer's Real Job: Future-Proofing the Film

If you are producing your first feature film, your primary responsibility is not just getting the film made. Your job is to make sure that:

1. The script you choose can realistically be financed
2. The film can still be sold when it is finished
3. The project has at least a *chance* of making its money back

That means thinking far beyond what is popular *right now*.

One of the most common mistakes first-time producers make is choosing a script based on current market trends without considering how long it actually takes to make a film. Development alone can take one to two years. Add financing, production, post-production, and sales, and you are easily looking at two to three years before your film is finished and ready to sell.

A producer must constantly ask:

- Is this genre cyclical or trend-driven?
- How many similar films are being made right now?
- Who is still buying this *two years from now*?

Ignoring these questions doesn't just reduce your chances of success, it can quietly kill your film before it ever has a chance.

Let me give you a dose of reality:

Take a film like *Mad Max*, for example. Yes, it was a massive success, but it was also a once-in-a-lifetime anomaly. While it is tempting to hope your first feature will follow in its footsteps, the odds are heavily against it. Even if your film is good, sometimes even if it is great, selling it is still an uphill battle. That is why it is critical to think about your target market and distribution strategy before you even write the script.

Understand the Film Market

The first step in preparing for your first feature film is understanding how the film market operates. Most filmmakers approach this business backward. They write a script they are passionate about, cobble together funding, shoot the film, and then start thinking about how to sell it. By then, it is often too late.

Here is what you should do instead: research the market first. What genres are currently in demand? What types of films are buyers looking for? Which films tend to sell well, and why? These are questions you need to answer before you write a single word of your script.

For example, Christmas romantic comedies are consistently one of the most sought-after genres in the industry. I knew this when I decided to make *Twelve Toys of Christmas*. I did not make the film because I had a personal passion for holiday romances. I made it because I knew there was a market for it. One acquisitions executive told me that even if a Christmas romantic comedy is bad, it is still sellable. That said, even with a good film in a popular genre, selling it is not guaranteed. I spent twelve months pitching *Twelve Toys of Christmas* to distributors and still struggled to secure deals.

When it comes to selling your film, there are two main types of distribution deals you need to understand: revenue share deals and buyout deals.

Revenue Share Deals

In a revenue share deal, the distributor takes your film, pays you a minimum guarantee (MG), essentially an advance, and then gives you a percentage of the revenue the film generates. For example, one offer I received for *Twelve Toys of Christmas* included a $15,000 MG with a 35% revenue share. That means the distributor would keep 35% of the profits, and I would receive the remaining 65% on all future income after the MG has been paid back.

However, not all revenue share deals include an MG. In these cases, you are giving away the rights to your film for a set period of time for a certain territory without receiving any money upfront, and you are completely dependent on the distributor's ability to sell your film. This is a risky scenario, as you might not see any revenue for months or even years.

Buyout Deals

In a buyout deal, the distributor pays you a lump sum for the rights to your film. After that, you do not receive any additional revenue, no matter how successful the film becomes. While this can be a strong option if the upfront payment covers your costs, it also means you miss out on potential profits if your film becomes a hit.

The Importance of Documentation

Another critical aspect of selling your film is keeping your documentation in order. As a sales agent, I represented a film that had significant potential with a US distributor. The deal fell apart because the filmmaker had moved and lost essential paperwork. Years of work, countless hours, and a large financial investment were wasted because the documentation was not properly organized.

This is non-negotiable. You need to have every contract, release form, and piece of documentation securely stored and readily accessible. Distributors will demand proof of ownership, actor releases, music clearances, and more. If you cannot provide these, you will not be able to sell your film.

Why Contracts and Deliverables Affect Development (Not Just Sales)

Another critical mistake first-time producers make is assuming that contracts and deliverables only matter after the film is finished.

They do not.

Distributor contracts, deliverable requirements, and licensing terms should influence decisions made during development and production. If you do not understand these requirements early, you can accidentally make choices that later become extremely expensive or even deal-breaking. Let me give you a real example.

During production, we used licensed stock music and video assets from Artlist. Like many filmmakers, we assumed that the standard license covered everything. At the time, it seemed reasonable. After all, the content was licensed for commercial use. Then we received the distributor's contract. The distributor required physical media rights: DVD and Blu-ray. Yes, those still exist, and yes, distributors still ask for them. What we did not know was that physical media rights were not covered under the standard license we had used. When we contacted Artlist, we were told that clearing physical media rights for all assets used, around 25 tracks, would cost approximately $25,000 USD.

That single oversight nearly killed the deal.

Suddenly, a decision that seemed minor during production had massive financial consequences at the sales stage. In the end, we were able to negotiate a much lower fee, but it still hurt our finances badly. More importantly, it highlighted how dangerous it is to assume anything when it comes to licensing. This is why producers must understand distributor expectations before shooting:

- Music licenses
- Stock footage licenses
- Archival material: Logos, artwork, and signage
- Physical and digital media rights

A small misunderstanding can cost you tens of thousands of dollars or make a deal financially pointless.

Alternative Distribution Options: FilmHub

If you are struggling to find a traditional distributor, platforms like FilmHub offer another option. FilmHub is a digital distribution platform where you can upload your film along with all the necessary assets, such as posters and contracts, and make it available on a wide range of platforms like Amazon Prime, Tubi and Roku. FilmHub operates on a non-exclusive basis, meaning you retain the rights to your film and can distribute it in multiple territories.

FilmHub takes a 20% commission on any revenue generated by your film, which is lower than the commission typically charged by sales agents. However, they do not actively market your film, so it is up to you to promote it and drive viewership. If you decide to use a platform like FilmHub, make sure to set aside a portion of your budget for marketing. Also, once you distribute your film on FilmHub, you will not be able to grant another distributor exclusive rights, as you have already given those rights away. There is no way back.

2nd Edition (January 2026) UPDATE!... Distribution Platforms Are Not Stable Either: The FilmHub Example

Even distribution platforms that once seemed filmmaker-friendly are changing rapidly. Since the first edition of this book, FilmHub has significantly changed its business model. Reporting features that were previously available to filmmakers for free are now locked behind a PRO account, which, at the time of writing, costs $999 USD per year.

For many independent filmmakers, that is a substantial and unexpected expense, especially for a platform that previously positioned itself as a free alternative to traditional distribution.

Naturally, this change has caused significant backlash within the filmmaking community, and it remains to be seen how it will play out long term.

At this stage, my advice is cautious:

FilmHub can still be useful if you are self-distributing your own film and do not need to prepare detailed reports for investors or partners. However, if you are accountable to multiple stakeholders, limited reporting access can become a serious problem.

The takeaway is simple:
No platform is permanent. No business model is guaranteed. Producers must constantly reassess their distribution strategies.

Additional Tips for Marketability

If you want to increase your chances of selling your film, here are a few additional tips:

1. Choose the Right Genre

Focus on genres with proven markets. Christmas movies, horror films, and thrillers with female leads are often in demand.

2. Shoot in English

The English-language market is significantly larger than non-English markets. If possible, shoot your film in English to maximize its appeal.

3. Cast a Recognizable Actor

Even casting a moderately well-known actor for a day or two can significantly boost your film's marketability. Their name on your poster or in your trailer can make a world of difference.

Marketing has changed dramatically since the first edition of this book. Facebook is no longer the dominant force it once was. Instagram has largely taken over as a primary communication platform, and TikTok now dominates attention, especially among younger audiences. The amount of time people spend on TikTok is staggering, and its influence on what people watch, buy, and talk about cannot be ignored. For many films, TikTok now plays a larger role in discoverability than traditional advertising ever did.

This does not mean you need to become a TikTok expert overnight, but it does mean producers can no longer rely on outdated marketing assumptions. Understanding where audiences actually spend their time is now part of the producer's job.

Expect the Unexpected

Finally, no matter how well you prepare, unexpected challenges will arise. Actors might drop out, equipment might fail, or the weather might disrupt your schedule. These problems are inevitable, so it is essential to remain flexible and think on your feet.

For instance, I once had an actor cancel five minutes before production began on a short film. Thankfully, another actor knew someone who could step in, and we managed to keep the shoot on track. Moments like these will test your resolve, but they are also an integral part of the filmmaking process.

By learning the business of filmmaking and preparing for the challenges ahead, you will be in a much better position to succeed with your first feature. Remember, making the film is just the beginning. The real work begins when it is time to sell.

A Brief Note on AI (Because You Can't Ignore It)

AI has also evolved significantly since the first edition of this book.

Used correctly, AI can now assist producers with:

- Development research
- Pitch materials
- Marketing assets, Scheduling, and planning
- Early audience testing concepts

Used incorrectly, it can waste time or create false confidence.

This book will not turn you into an AI expert, but you should understand that AI is now a practical tool, not a novelty. Producers who learn to use it wisely will have a clear advantage over those who ignore it.

Actually making a film with AI is a completely new and evolving concept that will take time to mature, but one thing is certain: it will happen.

The Core Lesson

Most first-time filmmakers fail not because they aren't talented but because they don't think far enough ahead.

A producer must constantly look forward:

- To where the market is going, not where it is now
- To what distributors will demand, not what feels convenient today
- How small decisions during production can have massive consequences later

Making the film is only part of the job. Making a film that *can survive the market when it's finished* is the real challenge.

CHAPTER 5

WHAT TO DO, WAY BEFORE SHOOTING YOUR FILM?

In this chapter, I want to talk about the fundamentals, what you need to have in place before you seriously consider shooting your first feature film. This is not about cameras, lenses, or crew. It is about mindset, strategy, and understanding what you are truly committing to.

This is also where I need to update something I discussed in the first edition, at the time of writing, I believed I had secured a deal for the film. We had received a Letter of Intent, discussions had progressed, and everyone involved, including the sales agent and myself, believed the sale would go through. As you now know from the updated introduction, that deal eventually collapsed.

What matters here is not the disappointment, but the lesson.

Even with a strong genre, a completed film, a sales agent, and apparent buyer interest, nothing is guaranteed until contracts are signed and money changes hands. That experience reinforced the single most important rule I can give you as a producer:

Do not start making a film unless you understand exactly what will happen when it is completed.

Let me say that again, because it matters more than anything else in this book.

Do not start making a film unless you know what you are going to do with it once it is done.

This does not mean you need a signed distribution contract before you shoot, although that would be ideal. It means you must have a realistic, informed plan for how the film could be sold, who might buy it, what they will require from you, and what risks you are taking if that plan does not work out.

In the first edition, I spoke about having a plan, but I had not yet lived through a deal falling apart after it appeared secure. I have now. That experience sharpened my understanding of how brutal and unpredictable this industry can be.

When the first deal fell through, it was not because the film suddenly became bad. It was not because the genre no longer existed. It was a business decision made by people who owed us nothing beyond the contract they ultimately chose not to sign. That is the reality of this business.

The good news is that we eventually secured another deal. It came later, for slightly less money and with tougher financial consequences, but the film was distributed. The process of getting from "almost sold" to "actually sold" taught me more than the first deal ever could.

This is why everything you do before shooting matters so much.

Experience is essential. I am still assuming that if you are reading this book, you have already made short films, worked with crews, and experienced at least some level of production chaos. If you have not, stop here and go get that experience first. A feature film magnifies every problem you have faced on a short, financial, emotional, and legal level.

But experience alone is not enough.

You also need to understand that development is not just about polishing a script. Development is about positioning a project so that it still makes sense years later, when it finally reaches the market. Films rarely move fast. You are always making decisions in the present for a future you cannot fully control.

This is where many first-time producers get into trouble.

You cannot control the market, but you can prepare for volatility.

Part of that preparation is understanding distributor expectations before you shoot, not after. Distributor contracts, deliverables, licensing requirements, and insurance obligations all shape what you should and should not do during development and production.

If you do not understand these requirements early, you may make decisions that cost you serious money later or prevent you from closing a deal entirely. Music licensing, stock footage, archive material, artwork, logos, and physical media rights are not abstract legal concepts. They are real costs that can appear at the worst possible moment.

I learned this the hard way.

In the first edition, I spoke about being careful. In this edition, I am telling you that ignorance is not an excuse the market will accept. Buyers do not care that you "did not know." They only care whether your film is fully cleared, fully deliverable, and financially viable for them.

This is also why you must be emotionally prepared for uncertainty.

Even with planning, even with experience, even with professional representation, deals can fall apart. That does not mean you failed. It means you are operating in a business where control is limited, and outcomes are never guaranteed.

What matters is whether you have structured your project in a way that allows you to survive those setbacks.

So before you shoot your first feature film, ask yourself some hard questions:

Do I understand how this film could realistically be sold?

Do I know what buyers will require from me?

Do I understand the legal and financial consequences of the decisions I am making now?

Am I prepared, financially and mentally, if this takes longer than expected?

If you cannot answer those questions honestly, you are not ready yet.

And that is okay.

There is no prize for rushing into a feature film unprepared. There is only stress, debt, and regret.

Take your time. Learn the business side as deeply as you learn the creative side. Making the film is only the beginning, and what happens after can be far more difficult than anything that happens on set.

Why Selling a Film Is So Difficult

The market is volatile, constantly shifting based on trends, economic conditions, and the preferences of distributors. Even if you make something in a popular genre, as I did, there are no guarantees. Platforms might pass for reasons that have nothing to do with the quality of your film. They may already have a slate full of similar projects, or they might not see a strong marketing hook to sell your film to their audience. The reality is that the market often values commercial potential over artistic merit. That does not mean your film has to be a cookie-cutter product, but it does mean you need to be savvy about how it fits into the industry landscape.

The Lesson: Think About Distribution From Day One

I had a potential buyer for my film, but not a contract, only a letter of intent to purchase, which meant they could easily walk away. This was a mistake, but I understand their position. Distributors are very risk-averse. There was no guarantee of the film's quality, and there was no guarantee it would be completed on time. It was our first feature project, so we had to take the risk ourselves.

Here is what I've learned:

1. Know Your Market: Research the type of films distributors and platforms are buying. What's trending? What's oversaturated?

2. Build Relationships Early: Talk to sales agents and distributors before you start shooting. Show them your concept, your cast, and your vision.

3. Create a Marketing Hook: Your film needs a unique selling point and a way to stand out in a crowded market. Maybe it's a fresh twist on a familiar genre, a unique cultural perspective, or a big name in the cast.

4. Be Flexible: Sometimes, you need to pivot. If your first plan doesn't pan out, don't be afraid to explore new strategies, even if it means waiting longer than you'd like.

The Emotional Toll

I will not sugarcoat it: trying to sell your film is exhausting, both mentally and emotionally. You will face rejection, sometimes for reasons beyond your control. You will second-guess your decisions and wonder if you should have taken that less-than-ideal deal just to get it over with.

But perseverance pays off. If you have done your homework, stayed patient, and been strategic about your approach, you will eventually find the right home for your film.

Moving Forward

The experience of selling my first film taught me lessons I will carry into every project I will take on going forward. It is not just about creating something great. It is about knowing how to position it in a competitive market. While the process is grueling, there is nothing quite like the moment when you finally land that deal and see your work released into the world.

So as you embark on your filmmaking journey, remember this: always keep one eye on the creative process and the other on the business side. Filmmaking is an art, but it is also a business, and success requires mastering both.

Understanding the Market

The film market has undergone massive changes in the past few years. Between the pandemic, industry strikes, and the rise of VOD (Video on Demand) platforms, the landscape for selling films is entirely different now, then it was only a few years ago and it is constantly changing.

It began with the subscription model Netflix introduced, which disrupted the industry by creating a new way to consume content. Now every major studio, including Paramount, Apple, and Disney, wants to be the next Netflix. The result is a saturated market of subscription-based platforms, all competing for attention.

This oversaturation makes it incredibly difficult to predict where your film will fit. Add to that the constant shifts in consumer behavior, and you have a highly uncertain environment.

How to Prepare

So, how can you give yourself the best chance of success? Here are a few tips:

1. Spend as Little as Possible:

The lower your production costs, the lower the pressure to sell your film at a high price. This does not mean cutting corners on quality, but being smart with your budget can significantly improve your chances of making a profit.

2. Understand Market Demand:

Research the types of films that are currently in demand. For example, Christmas romantic comedies are usually a safe bet because they have a built-in audience. Horror is another genre that often sells well, especially in international markets.

3. Have a Sales Strategy Before You Shoot:

Before you roll the camera, think about who you are making this film for. Which distributors or platforms would be interested? What is your target audience? You need to have answers to these questions early on.

4. Be Realistic About the Market:

Remember, even with a great product, selling a film is an uphill battle. The industry is flooded with content, and you will need to stand out, not just with a good film, but with a solid plan to market and pitch it.

The Takeaway

Making a feature film is one of the most rewarding things you can do, but it is also one of the hardest. Having a finished film is only half the battle. Selling it is the other, often more difficult, half. In upcoming chapters, I will dive deeper into budgeting, market research, and sales strategies to help you navigate this challenging landscape. For now, remember this: start small, spend wisely, and always have a plan for your film's future.

CHAPTER 6

CHOOSING THE RIGHT FILM TO MAKE

Let us talk about a question that can truly make or break your production: what kind of film should you make?

This decision matters more than most first-time filmmakers realize. Choosing the wrong project can cost you years of work, large amounts of money, and, if you are unlucky, your appetite for filmmaking altogether. Choosing the right one will not guarantee success, but it will dramatically increase your chances of getting the film made, sold, and seen.

With the right mix of strategy, creativity, and market awareness, this decision becomes far less overwhelming and far more practical.

(Updated for Today's Market, 2026)

Step 1: What Language Should You Make Your Film In?

Language is one of the most important strategic decisions you will make early on.

If your goal is international sales, English remains the dominant language of film and television distribution worldwide. Films in

English are easier to market, easier to subtitle, and generally easier for distributors to place across multiple territories.

That said, making a film in your native language is absolutely valid, but it comes with additional considerations. You need to think early about subtitles, dubbing, and how your story will translate culturally. AI-assisted dubbing has improved significantly in recent years and is now a realistic option for some projects, but it still comes with limitations and costs.

The key question is not, "What language do I want to shoot in?"

It is, "Can this film travel beyond my local market?"

If the answer is yes, then accessibility needs to be part of your development process, not an afterthought.

You will also have to make sure that you have a strong local distributor who will buy your film and hopefully government support as well.

Step 2: Genre Still Matters But Timing Matters More

Genre has always been one of the biggest drivers of sales, and that has not changed. What has changed is how quickly markets saturate and move on.

A genre that is easy to sell today may be extremely difficult to sell by the time your film is finished, especially when development and production can take two to three years.

This is where producers need to think ahead, not sideways.

Romantic Comedies

Romantic comedies, particularly holiday-themed ones, remain popular with broadcasters and streaming platforms. There is consistent demand, especially in North and South America, and audiences understand the format.

The downside is saturation. When too many similar films flood the market, distributors become very selective. If your romantic comedy does not clearly meet expectations or offer a recognizable hook, it may struggle, even if it is well-made.

Horror

Horror continues to be one of the strongest genres for low-budget filmmakers. It travels well internationally, does not rely heavily on star power, and can be made effectively with limited resources.

The challenge is competition. Horror is crowded, and originality is essential. Buyers are no longer impressed by "another horror film." They want a concept they can sell in one sentence.

Thrillers

Thrillers sit somewhere in the middle. They appeal to a wide audience and work well internationally, but they often require higher production value to feel convincing. Multiple locations, complex plot mechanics, and sustained tension all add pressure to a low budget.

Action

Action remains popular, but it is one of the riskiest genres for first-time producers. Expectations are high, safety requirements are strict, and costs escalate quickly. Unless you have a clever, contained approach, action films are rarely forgiving at the low-budget level.

A New Reality: Vertical Content and Short-Form Storytelling

One of the biggest shifts since the first edition of this book is the rapid rise of vertical content.

Short-form, vertically shot drama and narrative content designed for mobile viewing has exploded, driven largely by platforms like

TikTok and other mobile-first ecosystems. In some regions, vertical drama series are being financed, produced, and monetized faster than traditional independent features.

This does not mean feature films are dead. Far from it, but it does mean producers now have more options and more competition for attention.

Vertical content changes several assumptions:

- Stories are shorter and more immediate
- Production timelines are faster.
- Budgets are smaller, but volume is higher.
- Audience engagement happens in real time.

For some producers, especially first-timers, vertical content can be a lower-risk entry point into storytelling, audience building, and monetization. For others, it can become a marketing tool that supports a traditional feature or series.

The key takeaway is this: you can no longer ignore format when choosing what to make. Screen size, viewing habits, and attention spans are now part of both the creative and business equation.

Step 3: Market Research Is No Longer Optional

Once you have narrowed down a genre and format, research becomes critical.

Talk to distributors. Talk to sales agents. Ask what they are actually buying, not what they bought two years ago. Markets shift quickly, and decisions made early in development must be based on current demand, not historical trends.

You should also understand where your audience is likely to discover your film. Marketing has shifted dramatically. Facebook is no longer the dominant force it once was. Instagram has taken over as the primary communication platform for many filmmakers, and short-form video has become essential for awareness.

If you do not think about marketing until your film is finished, you are already behind.

Step 4: The Script Still Comes First But Context Matters

No trend, genre, or platform can save a weak script.

Everything still starts on the page.

A strong script does not just tell a good story. It understands its audience, its format, and its limitations. It recognizes what it can realistically achieve within a reasonable budget and timeline.

Getting honest feedback is essential. Writers and producers are often too close to the material to see its flaws. Outside opinions, especially from people who understand both storytelling and the market, are invaluable.

Platforms like Stage 32 can be useful for connecting with other filmmakers, writers, and consultants, but feedback is only helpful if you are willing to hear it. Rewriting is not failure. It is part of the process.

Your first draft is rarely your best draft.

Final Thoughts

Choosing the right film to make today is no longer just about taste or passion. It is about timing, format, audience behavior, and understanding where the industry is heading, not where it has been.

Whether you are making a feature film, exploring vertical storytelling, or combining both, the goal remains the same: create something that excites you creatively and has a realistic path to an audience.

Passion will keep you going.

Strategy will keep you solvent.

Choose wisely, develop carefully, and remember that every decision you make now will echo years down the line, when your film is finally ready to meet the market.

CHAPTER 7

FINANCING YOUR FILM

Making a film is an incredible adventure. It is thrilling, creative, and one of the most satisfying things you will ever do, but it is also a financial puzzle. Figuring out your budget is one of the first steps on this journey, and it is crucial to get it right. It can make or break your film. Do not worry. This is your chance to dream big and get practical.

Let us dive into how you can set your budget, raise the money, and keep your project moving forward without losing your mind or your friends.

Figuring Out Your Budget

Your budget is not just a number. It is the blueprint for what your film can be. How much you need depends on several factors:

Genre

Some genres are naturally more budget-friendly. Horror, for example, is famous for being achievable on a shoestring budget, think *The Blair Witch Project* or *Paranormal Activity*. On the other hand, if you are aiming for a fast-paced action film, be prepared for a higher price tag because of fight scenes, stunts, and props.

Locations

Can you set your story in one primary location? If so, great. That will save you thousands. If your script requires multiple settings, expect costs to increase.

Cast and Crew

Want A-list actors? That is great, but you will need a substantial budget, a strong script, and likely an experienced partner. If you are working with limited funds, consider casting up-and-coming actors or local talent. You might also look at recognizable talent from a television series, someone who has visibility but does not yet command a premium fee.

Post-Production and Marketing

This is a major area. You will need funding for editing, sound design, and visual effects. Once the film is complete, how will you let people know about it? Posters, trailers, and social media ads all require funding. Do not leave this part out!

Start Small and Build Smart

Here's the trick: Start with a number you think you can realistically raise. Let's say you want to make a horror film for $100,000. Ask yourself:

- Can I actually raise $100,000?
- How long will it take to gather that money?
- Will my cast and crew still be available when I finally hit my goal?

If $100,000 feels too far out of reach, maybe $50,000 is more realistic. That's okay! Your first film doesn't need to have Hollywood-style explosions. Keep it simple, keep it focused, and you'll have a great shot at making something amazing.

Raising the Money

Fundraising is the part of filmmaking that few people like to talk about, but it is where the process truly begins. Do not worry. You have options, and with a little creativity, you will get there.

Friends and Family

This might feel like an awkward place to start, but trust me, it works. The people who already know and love you are often the most likely to believe in your dream.

Here's how to approach them:

• Be Honest: Let them know filmmaking is risky. There's a chance they might not see their money again or at least not for a long time.

• Write a Proposal: Lay it all out in a document what the film is about, why you're making it, and what their money will be used for. Make them feel like they're part of something special, because they are.

• Manage Expectations: Regular updates are key. Let your investors know how things are progressing, even if it's slow. This keeps the trust strong and helps avoid awkward conversations later.

Pro Tip: People don't always invest just for financial returns they invest in your dream. If your film showcases your community or highlights a cause they care about, that might be more important to them than the money.

Crowdfunding

Platforms like Kickstarter or Indiegogo can help you raise funds from people all over the world. But here's the thing: Crowdfunding takes work.

Build a Fan Base First

If you do not already have an audience, it will be difficult to reach people. Start building connections on social media, forums, or blogs to generate interest and excitement before you launch.

Offer Meaningful Rewards

Signed posters, shout-outs in the credits, and behind-the-scenes content are the kinds of perks that encourage people to contribute.

Stay Active

Crowdfunding is a full-time commitment while it is live. You will need to promote it every day, so make sure you have the time and energy to follow through.

Personal Investment

There is an old rule in the filmmaking world: "Never put your own money into your film." While that is smart advice, some filmmakers choose to break it carefully.

If you decide to invest your own money, treat it like a donation to the dream. Only invest what you can afford to lose, and remember that your time, effort, and passion are already significant investments in the project.

Loans

Should you take out a loan to fund your film? In most cases, no. Banks do not care about your dreams, and they will not wait patiently if your film does not generate revenue right away. If you are tempted to go this route, think carefully about the risks.

Tax Rebates and Film Incentives

This is where things get exciting. Many countries (and some U.S. states) offer tax rebates for filmmakers, meaning you can get a chunk of your money back after production.

• How It Works:

If your country offers a 30% rebate, and you spend $100,000 on your film, you can claim $30,000 back after production just for following their guidelines. This is a very dumbed-down explanation, of course, so you should look at each country and the US states' incentives closely and carefully.

• What You Need to Do:

Rebates often require paperwork, such as registering your production, keeping receipts, and hiring a local crew. It's worth the effort for the financial boost it can provide.

• Do Your Research:

Look up your country's or state's film office to find out what programs are available. Even a small rebate can make a big difference.

Tips to Keep Your Film on Track

1. Budget for the Unexpected:

Something *always* costs more than you planned. Build a cushion into your budget so you're not scrambling later.

2. Focus on Simplicity:

A great story told with limited resources will always beat an over-ambitious project that falls short.

3. Keep Your Investors Updated:

Whether it's your family, friends, or crowdfunding backers, let them know how the project is going. They'll appreciate being part of the journey.

4. Don't Skimp on Marketing:

The best film in the world won't succeed if no one knows about it. Save some cash for posters, social media ads, and festival submissions.

Final Thoughts

Raising money for a film can feel daunting, but this is the beginning of your dream becoming a reality. Be honest, be resourceful, and do not be afraid to get creative. Every great filmmaker started somewhere, and this is your moment to take the first step.

Filmmaking is a demanding journey, but it is worth every second. Stay persistent, stay focused, and go make your movie. You have this!

UPDATE!... Be very clear to your investors with regard to the disbursement of monies. There are usually three situations that will arise:

You do not sell the film

This is the worst-case scenario, and it does happen. The financial outcome is simple: no one gets paid.

You sell the film under a revenue share deal or place it on a platform

With this option, you receive an unknown amount of money over time, often trickling in across several years. If you choose this route, you will have a "waterfall" structure in place, meaning participants are paid according to agreed priorities once revenue is received. How much each party earns depends entirely on the agreements you have negotiated.

You sell the film outright for a lump sum

This can be a strong outcome, but do not assume you will receive all the money at once. Every deal is different, but a common structure might include 10% upon signing the contract, 10% upon delivery, 30% upon release, and 50% six months after release. Your waterfall will reflect this payment structure.

CHAPTER 8

FINDING PROFESSIONAL INVESTORS

Let us talk about investors. This is one of the most important and most misunderstood parts of filmmaking.

Films do not fund themselves. Whether you are making a small independent feature or something more ambitious, at some point you will need other people's money. That means approaching investors, and it means taking on responsibility, not just creatively, but ethically and financially.

Those investors might be friends or family. They might be local business owners. Or they might be professional investors who understand risk and diversification. Whoever they are, you need to enter these conversations prepared, honest, and realistic.

The starting point is always the same: an investor proposal document.

What Is an Investor Proposal Document?

Think of this document as your written pitch. It explains who you are, what you are making, how much money you are raising, how that money will be used, and, most importantly, how investors might get their money back.

But this is not just a financial document.

People rarely invest in films purely for financial reasons. The risks are high, the timelines are long, and there are far safer ways to make money. Investors usually come on board because they believe in you, the project, or the experience of being involved.

Your proposal should reflect that.

It should clearly communicate:

- Why are you making this film
- Why *now* is the right time
- Why are you the person to do it

And yes, it should also explain the risks clearly and without sugar-coating them.

Be Honest About Risk Even When It Gets Uncomfortable

This is where I need to be very honest about my own experience.

In the first edition of this book, I spoke about offering investors a return that included a premium. In my case, I promised my investors their money back, plus an additional percentage once the film sold. That was the plan, and at the time, it was based on realistic expectations.

What actually happened was more complicated.

When the film finally sold, the amount we received was not enough to repay everyone their full investment plus the promised interest. That is a difficult sentence to write, but it is an important one.

This is not something producers like to discuss. But it happens.

What matters is not pretending this risk does not exist. What matters is how you handle it when it becomes reality.

From the very beginning, my investors were kept informed. We had regular conversations, meetings, and lunches. They knew how long the process was taking, what offers were coming in, which deals fell through, and what challenges we were facing. There were no surprises.

When it became clear that I would not be able to repay the full investment plus interest, I did not avoid the issue. I communicated with them directly. I explained exactly what had happened, why it had happened, and what the realistic outcome would be.

Every investor was given:

- Full transparency
- Detailed spreadsheets
- Exact figures showing income, expenses, commissions, and deductions
- A clear breakdown of what money had come in and where it went

I made it clear that any income generated by the film would be paid out to investors, even if it meant that I personally recovered nothing.

This level of transparency is not optional. It is the only way to look investors in the eye, maintain your integrity, and preserve the possibility of working with them again in the future.

You have very little control over outcomes in this industry.

You can control honesty, communication, and respect.

Staying in Touch Is Not Optional

One of the biggest mistakes first-time producers make is disappearing after the money is raised.

Investors do not want silence. Silence creates anxiety, distrust, and resentment. Regular communication builds confidence, even when the news is not good.

In my case, investors always knew:

- Who I was talking to.
- What stage were sales discussions at.
- What offers had we received? Why were decisions being made.

This wasn't about reassuring them; it was about respecting the fact that this was *their money.*

If you ever want to raise money again, your reputation will matter more than your last film's performance.

A Reality Check: How Professional Investors Think

Professional investors approach films very differently from friends or family.

They generally:

- Expect risk
- Understand that not every project returns capital. Diversify across multiple investments
- Focus on structure, not emotion

Professional investors usually want clarity on:

- Recoupment order Profit waterfalls
- Legal protection, Reporting and transparency

They are less interested in vague promises and more interested in whether the deal is structured sensibly. Many professional investors assume that a film may not return their capital at all, and they factor that risk into their decision.

This does not mean they are indifferent if things go wrong. It means they care more about whether you handle the situation professionally.

A producer who communicates clearly, provides proper documentation, and takes responsibility, even when outcomes are disappointing, is far more likely to be trusted again than someone who overpromises and avoids difficult conversations.

What Should Be in the Proposal?

Your investor proposal does not need to be long. Mine was six pages. It was clean, visual, and direct.

It included:

- A short introduction about me and why I was making the film
- A clear description of the project
- A realistic budget overview
- A discussion of distribution strategy
- A transparent explanation of risk
- Investor perks that made participation feel meaningful

Visual material helped, concept images, stills from previous work, and mood references. These are not gimmicks. They help investors *see* what they are backing.

The Bottom Line

Raising money for a film is not just about selling a dream. It is about accepting responsibility.

You are asking people to trust you with their money. That trust does not end when the check clears. It lasts until the project is finished and fully accounted for.

Sometimes things go exactly as planned.

Sometimes they do not.

What defines you as a producer is not whether everything works perfectly, but whether you remain honest, transparent, and accountable when it does not.

If you do that, you may not only protect your reputation but also earn the opportunity to work with the same investors again, even after a difficult outcome.

In this industry, that trust is worth more than any single deal.

How film finance works in plain English.

If you have never had the opportunity to be involved in finance before, the way films are funded can feel confusing, intimidating, and overly complicated. That is normal. Even people who have worked in the industry for years sometimes struggle to explain it clearly.

So let us strip it back.

The easiest way to understand film finance is to stop thinking about it as "film money" and start thinking about it the same way you would think about buying a house or a car.

Think of a film like a house.

Very few people buy a house with cash.

Instead, you usually use a combination of:

- Your own money (your deposit)
- A mortgage from a bank
- Sometimes, additional loans or incentives

A film works in a very similar way.

Your equity investors are like the people putting down the deposit.

Banks and lenders are like the mortgage providers.

Tax incentives, subsidies, or pre-sales are like government grants or rebates.

And just like with a house, not all money is treated equally.

Equity: The Riskiest Money in the Film

Equity is the money that takes the biggest risk.

Using the house example, equity is like your personal savings. If everything goes well, you benefit. If things go badly, this is the money that gets hit first.

In a film:

- Equity investors put in cash
- They usually get paid last
- If the film underperforms, they may not get all their money back

This is why equity is risky and why you must never pretend otherwise when talking to investors.

Loans: Money That Gets Paid Back First

When you take out a home loan or a car loan, the bank does not care how emotionally attached you are to the house or the car. They care about repayment.

Film lenders are the same.

If a bank or lender puts money into your film, they expect:

- Clear contracts
- Security
- And to be paid back before anyone makes a profit

This is important:

Lenders are not investors. They are not sharing the risk the same way.

Gap Financing: Borrowing Against the Future

Gap financing sounds complicated, but the idea is simple.

Imagine you are buying a house and believe that in two years, your salary will increase. A bank might agree to lend you a bit more money based on that projected income, but only if it is highly confident the increase will happen.

Gap loans in film work the same way.

A lender agrees to provide financing based on estimated future sales from territories your film has not yet sold. Those estimates usually come from a sales agent.

Lenders are cautious. They do not lend dollar for dollar.

If you want to borrow one dollar, they will typically want to see two to three dollars' worth of projected value.

That tells you something important:

- Gap loans are conservative
- They are not guaranteed
- And they must still be repaid even if sales disappoint

Mezzanine Loans: Somewhere in the Middle

Mezzanine finance sits between a bank loan and equity.

Think of it like a high-interest personal loan you take out *after* your mortgage is already in place. It's riskier for the lender, so it costs more.

In films, mezzanine lenders:

- Charge a higher interest rate
- Often ask for extra benefits (credits or backend points)
- Still get paid before equity

For first-time producers, mezzanine finance can be dangerous if not fully understood, because it adds pressure to the project.

Bridge Loans: Paying to Buy Time

Bridge loans exist to solve timing problems.

Imagine you are buying a house. Your mortgage is approved, but the money will not arrive for another few weeks. You might take a short-term loan to cover the gap.

That is a bridge loan.

In film, bridge loans are often used when production must begin, but other funds have not yet arrived. They are short-term and often expensive.

They are useful in emergencies, but they are not friendly money.

Who Gets Paid First?

This is the most important concept in this entire section.

When money comes in from a film sale, it does not get shared equally.

Just like with a house:

1. The bank gets paid first
2. Other lenders get paid next
3. Equity investors get paid last

If there isn't enough money to go around, the people at the bottom may get nothing.

This is why a film can "sell" and still not repay investors fully.

Why This Matters to You

You do not need to use complex finance on your first film.

But you do need to understand:

- That loans always get paid before investors
- That more debt means more pressure
- That equity carries the highest risk

If you don't understand this, you can't explain risk properly to investors and that's when trust breaks down.

The Simple Rule

If you remember only one thing, remember this: banks lend. Investors take risks. Producers are responsible for explaining the difference, and hope is not a financial plan.

Structure matters more than optimism.

Understanding this early will save you from very painful conversations later.

CHAPTER 9

FILM REBATES

THE ONLY "FREE MONEY" IN FILM (WITH CONDITIONS)

Film rebates are one of the few parts of film financing that can work in your favor if you understand them properly.

At its simplest, a film rebate is a system in which a country or region returns a percentage of the money you spend there. You spend first, then, after audits and approvals, you receive a portion of that money back.

If that sounds like a tax refund, that is because it essentially is one.

Think of a Film Rebate Like Cashback

The easiest way to understand a rebate is to think of cashback on a credit card. You spend money in approved ways, follow the rules, and later receive a percentage back.

But just like cashback schemes:

- Not all spending qualifies

- You must prove what you spent
- You only get the money *after* the purchase

Film rebates work the same way just on a much larger scale.

The Hungarian Model (Why So Many Films Shoot There)

Hungary is one of the strongest examples of how a film rebate system can attract international productions.

Under the Hungarian film incentive system, productions can receive a 30% rebate on eligible local spending. That includes things like:

- Hungarian cast and crew
- Local services
- Equipment rental
- Post-production done in Hungary

This is why so many international films and series choose to shoot or complete post-production there. From a producer's perspective, a rebate can cover a significant portion of the budget and dramatically reduce risk.

However, and this is critical, the rebate is not paid upfront. You must first finance the production, spend the money, complete the required audits, and only then is the rebate paid.

This means a rebate is not cash. It is a promise of future cash.

How Rebates Fit Into Film Financing

Because rebates are reliable in established territories, banks and lenders are often willing to lend against them. This is similar to how a bank might approve a loan, knowing your tax refund is coming.

But again, structure matters.

The rebate:

- Comes later
- Is usually pledged to a lender
- Often recoups before equity

This is why producers must understand rebates *before* locking budgets or making promises to investors.

Rebates Are Now Global, Not Regional

Hungary is far from alone.

Across the world, governments use film rebates to attract productions, boost local employment, and promote tourism.

In the United States, many states offer their own incentive programs. These vary widely in percentage, eligibility, and reliability. Some states offer refundable tax credits, others offer transferable credits, and some cap their programs annually, which means timing matters.

Across Europe, countries such as the United Kingdom, Ireland, Germany, and several Eastern European nations offer competitive incentives. Each system has its own rules, minimum spend requirements, and cultural tests.

More recently, the Middle East has entered the picture in a serious way. Countries such as the United Arab Emirates and others in the region now offer attractive rebates, modern infrastructure, and streamlined approval processes to attract international productions.

The big takeaway is this:

rebates are no longer a bonus; they are part of the financing strategy.

What Rebates Do Not Do

This is where first-time producers often get confused.
A rebate does not:

- Guarantee a profit
- Replace equity
- Eliminate risk
- Solve a weak sales strategy

A rebate reduces your net cost, but it does not magically make a film sellable. You can still make a film with a rebate and lose money.

Why Producers Must Understand Rebates Early

Rebates affect:

- Where you shoot
- Who you hire
- How you structure your budget
- When money flows back into the project

If you ignore rebates until late in development, you may discover that:

- You structured the budget incorrectly
- You hired the wrong people
- You missed eligibility thresholds
- You promised investors money that arrives much later than expected

Understanding rebates early allows you to design the film around financial reality not wishful thinking.

The Simple Truth About Rebates

If you remember nothing else, remember this:

A rebate lowers risk, but it does not remove it.

Used properly, rebates can make a project viable that otherwise would not be. Used poorly, they create false confidence and cash flow problems.

As a producer, your job is not just to chase the highest percentage. It is to understand when the money arrives, who controls it, and how it affects everyone else in the deal. That understanding starts long before the cameras roll.

CHAPTER 10

I HAVE A SCRIPT AND THE MONEY!...NOW WHAT?

The Value of Preparation

Preparation is your secret weapon. While the temptation to jump straight into production is strong, an underprepared project can fall apart at any stage, whether in financing, production, or distribution. The more thoroughly you prepare, the fewer surprises you will face and the better equipped you will be to handle challenges.

What Preparation Looks Like

• Market Research: Study the type of films similar to yours. Look into box office trends, audience preferences, and critical responses.

• Networking: Build relationships within the industry producers, directors, writers, and distributors. These connections can prove invaluable down the road.

• Legal and Business Foundations: Understand the contracts, intellectual property rights, and financing terms associated with filmmaking.

Taking the extra time to prepare is not a delay; it's an investment in your project's success.

Pitch Decks: Your Film's First Impression

What Makes a Great Pitch Deck?

1. Clear and Concise Content

• Keep it short 5–10 pages at most. People are busy, so get to the point quickly.

• Use bullet points, headings, and visuals to break up text.

2. Professional Design

• Font & Layout: Use clean, modern fonts and an uncluttered layout.

• Branding: If your project has a unique aesthetic (e.g., neon cyberpunk or gritty noir), let the pitch deck's design reflect that style.

• Color Scheme: Choose a color palette that suits the tone of your film. For instance, dark tones for horror, pastels for romantic comedy, or bold colors for action.

3. Compelling Visuals

• Incorporate AI-generated images or professionally designed artwork to bring your film's world to life.

• Use visual references from similar films to establish the mood and tone.

How to Make It Stand Out

• Unique Selling Points: Highlight what makes your project different. For example, is your horror film based on a chilling true story? Does your romantic comedy have a groundbreaking twist?

• Testimonials: If possible, include a quote from someone respected in the industry who has reviewed your project and supports it.

Why AI is a Game-Changer

How AI Helps Filmmakers

1. Visual Concepting - Generate high-quality images for your pitch deck or pre-visualization. For example, if your film is set on a futuristic Mars colony, AI can create a concept art version of your vision.

2. Writing Assistance - AI tools can help you polish your pitch deck, write dialogue, or even refine your script. This is especially useful for making your materials sound professional and engaging.

3. Video Teasers - Create short promotional reels or animatics to show potential collaborators what your film could look like. AI can help with video editing, effects, and even generating storyboards.

4. Saving Time - Delegate repetitive or time-consuming tasks to AI so you can focus on the creative and strategic aspects of filmmaking.

The Script: Your Bedrock

Why Script Development Is Crucial

A mediocre script can sink even the most well-funded and well-thought-out production. The script is the blueprint for your entire project, and every element, including direction, acting, cinematography, and even marketing, stems from it.

Steps to Refine Your Script

1. Get Feedback: Share your script with trusted colleagues or professional script readers. Platforms like Stage 32 or WeScreenplay can connect you with experts who will provide actionable insights.

2. Multiple Drafts: Don't settle for the first draft. Even seasoned screenwriters revise their work numerous times before the script is ready.

3. Research the Market: Before finalizing your script, make sure there's a demand for your type of story. Is your genre trending? Are audiences craving a fresh take on a specific theme?

4. Table Reads: Host a table read with actors to hear your dialogue spoken aloud. This can reveal pacing issues, clunky lines, or plot holes.

5. Most importantly, make sure that you have the budget necessary to shoot the film in your script. The writer has to be aware of budget constraints, and so does your director. Literally, everyone has to be on the same page! If you feel that the budget isn't there and no one wants to make compromises, cancel the production there and then!

Researching the Market

Why It Matters

Making a great film is not enough. You also need to make a film that people want to watch. Understanding the market will help you position your project effectively and improve your chances of success.

Key Areas to Research

1. Audience Preferences

• What genres are trending? For example, are audiences currently drawn to psychological horror over jump-scare horror?

• What are the demographics of your target audience (age, gender, geographic region, etc.)?

2. Industry Trends

• Are certain types of films or genres oversaturated?

• What are streamers like Netflix, Hulu, or Amazon looking for right now?

3. Competition

• Look at similar films. What worked? What didn't?

• Study box office numbers and critical reviews to learn from their successes and failures.

Approaching Distributors

How to Find the Right Distributor

1. Specialization: Most distributors focus on specific genres. A horror film distributor may not be the right fit for a romantic comedy.

2. Track Record: Look for distributors who have successfully marketed and sold films like yours.

3. Reputation: Research online reviews, testimonials, and feedback from other filmmakers who have worked with the distributor.

Making Contact

1. Initial Email or Meeting: Be concise. Introduce yourself, your project, and why you think it's a good fit for them. Attach your pitch deck, but keep the email short and professional.

2. Follow-Up: If you don't hear back after a couple of weeks, send a polite follow-up email. Persistence is key, but don't be pushy.

3. Building Relationships: Attend film markets and festivals where you can meet distributors face-to-face. Networking is often more effective than cold emails.

The Perfect Scenario

What Does Success Look Like?

• A distributor loves your pitch deck and requests the script.

• They see potential in your project and offer feedback or notes for improvement.

• You secure financing or distribution support based on their enthusiasm.

Tips to Maximize Your Chances

• Attach a well-known actor, director, or crew member to your project. Even a small name can make a big difference.

• Keep refining your pitch deck and script to ensure they are as strong as possible.

Final Thoughts

Getting your film ready for production is a marathon, not a sprint. Each step refining your script, creating a stellar pitch deck, researching the market, and approaching distributors requires time, effort, and attention to detail. But with thorough preparation and a clear plan, you'll be well on your way to making your dream film a reality.

CHAPTER 11

BUILDING YOUR TEAM

TIPS FOR ASSEMBLING THE RIGHT CAST, CREW, AND SUPPORT

So let us say you have your script polished, your funding is mostly in place, and you are ready to move into pre-production. This is where the project truly begins to come together, but it is also where things can become overwhelming. Do not worry. I will walk you through how to assemble a strong team to bring your vision to life, even on a tight budget.

First Steps: What Do You Already Have?

Some of you may already have a crew or even a cast in mind. You may have started thinking about who could help as soon as you began writing your script. That is great. But let us assume you are starting from scratch. Whether you are in a big city, a small town, or somewhere in between, there are many ways to find talented people to join your project.

Where to Find Your Team

1. Local Film Communities

• Film Clubs: Most cities, big or small, have local film clubs. These are full of people passionate about filmmaking, from hobbyists to aspiring professionals.

• Production Companies: Look for small production companies that create online content, corporate videos, or even wedding films. Many of these folks are itching to work on something more creative, like a feature film.

• Film Schools: Students are often eager to gain experience. Reach out to film schools or universities in your area and post opportunities for them to join your team.

Pro Tip: When reaching out to potential collaborators, make sure you're clear about the scope of the project, the budget (or lack thereof), and the timeline. Transparency goes a long way in building trust.

Set Clear Expectations

Before diving into the hiring process, you need to have two key documents ready:

1. Your Budget: Know exactly how much you can afford to spend on cast, crew, equipment, and locations.

2. Your Schedule: A low-budget feature film should ideally be shot in 10 to 15 days. This keeps costs down and makes scheduling easier for everyone involved.

Why so short?

Every additional day on set increases costs significantly, including gear rentals, meals, transportation, and wages. Scheduling more scenes within fewer days may require longer hours, but it is often far more cost-effective than extending your shoot.

Contracts: Protect Yourself and Your Film

This is critical. Every single person working on your film, whether they are being paid, working for free, or contributing in-kind services, needs to sign a contract.

Key Contract Types

1. Standard Contracts: For paid cast and crew.

2. In-Kind Agreements: For those donating their time, equipment, or expertise.

3. Profit-Share Agreements: If you can't pay upfront, you can offer a share of future profits. Make sure this is clearly defined in writing.

4. Deferred Payment Agreements: You pay a portion upfront and the rest after the film is sold.

Pro Tip: Always have a lawyer review your contracts to ensure everything is legally sound. Disputes can derail your film faster than you can imagine.

Actors: Finding the Right Talent

How to Cast Your Film

• Online Casting Platforms: Websites like StarNow or local casting directories can connect you with actors eager to work on indie projects.

• Film Schools: Many acting students are hungry for lead roles to showcase their range.

• Theatre groups: Almost all cities town will have theatre groups, and I can assure you, they will be thrilled to be allowed to feature in a film

• Pitch the Opportunity: Highlight the benefits of joining your film, such as a lead role in a feature or exposure to international markets.

Negotiating with Actors

Actors, especially those early in their careers, are often willing to take on projects with lower pay if the role offers something valuable to them:

- A lead role to show their acting range.
- A chance to work in a different country or genre.
- A script that excites them.

For example, for my Christmas rom-com, I secured a talented lead actress by offering her a fair (but reduced) rate, covering her travel and accommodation, and emphasizing the opportunity for her to star in a feature as a lead intended for the U.S. market. She loved the script, and the rest is history.

Getting Big-Name Talent (on a Budget!)

If you're working on your second or third film with a slightly bigger budget, you can sometimes snag a "name" actor for a day or two of shooting.

- Write the screenplay in a way that their scenes can be shot in just a day or two.
- Use their name and face in your marketing (with their permission in the contract).

This strategy can dramatically increase your film's marketability and value without blowing your budget.

Crew: Finding the Right People

Key Crew Members

Some roles are essential to get right:

1. Director of Photography (DP): They'll be responsible for how your film looks. Hire someone experienced or skilled, even if you have to stretch your budget slightly.

2. First Assistant Director (1st AD): They'll keep your set organized and ensure you stay on schedule.

3. Sound Engineer: Bad sound will ruin even the best-looking film. Don't cut corners here.

4. Line Producer / Production Manager - one of these crew members needs to have experience, as they are responsible for contracts and the budget, so unless you want to do this, make sure you have someone you can trust.

Where to Find Crew
• Film schools and universities.
• Local production companies.
• Freelance platforms or forums for filmmakers.

Partnerships: Working with Small Film Companies
If your script is strong, consider reaching out to smaller production companies. They may be willing to invest in your project, either with cash or with in-kind services such as equipment, post-production support, or marketing expertise.

Partnerships: Working with Friends, Acquaintances, or Family
If you are entering this project with partners, this is the moment to slow down and be completely clear with one another.

Partnerships can be incredibly powerful, but they are also one of the most common sources of conflict in filmmaking. The reason is almost always the same: expectations were never properly aligned at the beginning.

Before anything moves forward, you need to agree clearly and in detail on who is responsible for what, how decisions will be made, and how money will be divided. This applies to profit shares, fees, credits, and authority. The more specific you are now, the fewer problems you will face later.

This is not about mistrust. It is about clarity.

The single biggest issue I see in partnerships is imbalance. One person ends up doing far more work than expected, carrying the project through development, production, and sales, while the other partner remains less involved but still expects the same financial reward at the end. That situation rarely ends well.

If you do not define roles and responsibilities early, resentment builds quietly. And resentment does not disappear just because a film gets made or sold. It often surfaces when money finally arrives.

Treat partnerships for what they are: a business relationship. Be honest about time commitment, workload, and expectations. Put everything in writing. Make sure everyone understands that equal ownership does not automatically mean equal effort.

Getting this right at the start can save friendships, careers, and projects down the line.

Co-Productions

This is a great way to share the risk and resources while benefiting from people's experience and industry connections. Just make sure the partnership terms are clear and fair to everyone involved.

Final Thoughts: Building Relationships That Last

Making a film is a team effort, and the relationships you build along the way can lead to opportunities for future projects. Treat your cast and crew with respect, be clear about expectations, and do not forget to express your gratitude.

Remember that filmmaking is a marathon, not a sprint. Surround yourself with people who share your vision and are excited to bring your story to life.

In the following chapters, we will explore additional pre-production strategies, including directors, locations, and preparing for demanding but rewarding shoot days!

CHAPTER 12

CHOOSING YOUR DIRECTOR

ONE OF THE MOST IMPORTANT DECISIONS YOU WILL MAKE

Finding the right director can make or break your film. It is one of the most important decisions you will make as a producer, and I know this from experience, sometimes from difficult ones. Even mistakes, however, can teach valuable lessons.

Whether you are making a short film or stepping into your first feature, this decision deserves careful thought. The director will be the person guiding the creative vision. If they did not write the screenplay, they will still be responsible for translating it to the screen, working with actors, and shaping the film's look, tone, and overall feel.

As a producer, your responsibility is to position and sell the film. That means understanding what the project needs to look like, which elements it must include, and how much you can realistically afford to spend to bring it to life. If your director does not understand this, if they do not appreciate the business side of filmmaking, problems can escalate quickly.

The First Rule: Find a Director Who Gets It

When you're looking for a director, the very first thing to watch for is whether they understand the boundaries of the budget. You're going to lay out what you can afford, and if you get even the slightest sense that they're not listening or respecting that, it's time to walk away. No matter how talented they seem, if they're constantly asking for things that aren't in the budget, it's not going to work.

Here's the harsh truth: a director can sink your production if they don't respect the financial limits. The last thing you want is to end up with a film that's incomplete or wildly over budget because your director decided to push past your resources.

They need to understand the budget and have read the script thoroughly. If they're asking to spend more, you have to question whether they've truly thought it through. If they haven't, they've got to go.

Research, Research, Research

So, how do you find the right person? Start by looking at their previous work. Ideally, they have directed at least one feature film. If not, look for short films that demonstrate skill and creativity. Have they worked well with actors? Do they know how to bring a story to life within a defined budget?

If possible, speak with producers who have worked with them before. Other producers will be honest about their experience. Trust me, if they had a bad experience, they will tell you. You will not even have to ask.

Also, take the time to sit down with your potential director and make sure you are on the same wavelength. Lay out your vision for the film and your budget, and confirm that they are fully on board. A good director knows how to bring a film to life within the available resources. If they start saying things like, "Oh, but we will need more money for this, or that," alarm bells should start ringing.

Set Clear Expectations Early

Before you start filming, make sure the director has a crystal-clear understanding of what you want the movie to look and feel like. Use examples from other films, mood boards, or visual references to ensure you are aligned. Here is the key: stay present on set to make sure that vision is being executed. I learned this the hard way. On one project, I had too much on my plate and was not on set as often as I should have been. By the time I realized what was happening, things had already begun to veer off track.

So stay involved. Watch the dailies. Monitor what is being shot. If things are not moving in the right direction, address it immediately. Do not assume it will fix itself. If you have to, fire the director on the spot!

Ego Has No Place on Set

This is a big one. Whether it is the director, a cast member, a crew member, or anyone else on set, there is no room for egos. Filmmaking is a collaborative process, and every decision must be made with one goal in mind: what is best for the film.

If someone's ego is getting in the way, it is time to part ways quickly. That might sound harsh, but you have to think about the bigger picture. The movie comes first. Every decision, every dollar spent, and every moment on set must serve the film.

Why the Director Matters So Much

At the end of the day, the director will move on to their next project once the film is finished. They will not be there to help you sell it, market it, or deal with any fallout if the budget spirals out of control. That responsibility falls entirely on you. So make sure they deliver the film you need, one you can sell and one that fits within the resources you worked so hard to secure.

As a producer, you are the one carrying responsibility for the film's success or failure. The director's job is to bring the story to life, but it must be done in a way that aligns with the bigger picture. If they cannot or will not do that, it is not going to work.

The Bottom Line

Finding the right director is about more than hiring someone with talent. You are looking for a partner, someone who understands the constraints of the budget, respects your vision, and is willing to collaborate to get the film made.

Take your time. Do your research. Talk to their previous collaborators. If you sense any red flags, especially when it comes to respecting the budget, do not ignore them. The director can either be your greatest ally or your biggest headache, so choose wisely.

And remember, the most important thing is the film itself. Every decision you make has to serve the film. Keep that in mind, and you will be in a much stronger position to succeed.

CHAPTER 13

LOCATIONS

AVOIDING NIGHTMARES AND SETTING
YOURSELF UP FOR SUCCESS

Let's talk about locations, an essential yet often tricky part of filmmaking. While I am not going to give you a step-by-step guide to scouting locations, I do want to share some crucial lessons that can help you avoid the kinds of headaches that derail a production.

If you have done any filmmaking before, you already know that locations come with a host of unexpected challenges. Maybe you used a friend's backyard or a relative's flat for a short film. It might have worked out, but it probably was not without its hiccups. Now imagine that on a much larger scale, with a feature film. Things can spiral quickly. Do not worry. I have some advice to help you navigate this part of the process with confidence.

What makes a location actually work
(Not Just Look Good)

One of the biggest traps first-time filmmakers fall into is choosing locations based purely on how they look.

A location can be visually perfect and still be a complete nightmare to shoot in.

As a producer, your job is not to find the most beautiful location. It is to find the location that allows you to finish the film on time, on budget, and without sacrificing sound quality, crew morale, or your sanity.

Here are the things you must consider long before you say yes to any location.

Sound Will Make or Break You

Sound problems are the number one reason scenes become unusable, expensive to fix, or impossible to complete properly.

Before you lock a location, spend time there doing absolutely nothing. Just listen.

Is there traffic nearby? Trains? Aircraft flight paths? Church bells? Factories? Dogs? Neighbors who like mowing their lawn at 7 a.m.?

Also, pay attention to what is above you. Rain on a metal or tin roof can completely ruin dialogue. It might sound romantic on screen, but it is a nightmare for sound recording. Once the rain starts, you may be forced to stop shooting entirely.

If a location only works when the weather behaves perfectly, it is not a reliable location.

Parking Is Not a Small Detail

Parking is one of those things nobody thinks about until it becomes a problem and then it becomes a very big problem.

Ask yourself:

- Where will the crew park?
- Where will trucks unload?

- Where will the equipment be staged?
- Will neighbours complain or call the police?

If parking is difficult, everything slows down. Late call times, stressed crew, rushed setups, and overtime costs all follow. On low-budget films, especially, poor parking logistics quietly drain money and energy.

A location with easy access and parking is often worth far more than a slightly "better-looking" one.

Power, Power, Power

Never assume the available power will be sufficient.

Can the location handle lighting, monitors, charging stations, and catering equipment without blowing circuits? Where are the fuse boxes? How old is the wiring?

If you do not know the answers, you are taking a risk. Generators cost money. Power outages cost time. Both can destroy a shooting day.

Weather and Nature Are Not Your Friends

Exterior locations always come with risk, but even interiors are affected by weather.

Rain, wind, heat, and cold all impact:

- Sound
- Actor performance
- Crew efficiency
- Equipment reliability

Also look for things like trees that drop leaves, birds that appear at the same time every day, or nearby water that brings insects. These details seem small until continuity becomes a nightmare.

If a location only works under perfect conditions, assume those conditions will not happen.

Toilets, Holding Areas, and Reality

This may not sound glamorous, but it matters.

Where do people go to the bathroom?

Where do actors wait between setups?

Where does makeup take place?

Where is the wardrobe located?

If you do not have clear answers, the crew will improvise, and improvisation usually leads to inefficiency and frustration.

A comfortable crew works better, faster, and with fewer mistakes. A miserable crew costs you money.

Control Is Everything

Ask yourself how much control you really have over the location.

Can people walk in unexpectedly?

Can neighbours shut you down?

Can businesses suddenly change their minds?

A location that looks great but can't be controlled is a liability. Control means fewer interruptions, better sound, and safer working conditions.

Think Like a Producer, Not a Tourist

Every time you scout, ask yourself:

- Can we shoot here repeatedly without surprises?

- Can we come back tomorrow and get the same conditions?
- What could realistically go wrong?

If you can answer those questions honestly, you're choosing locations like a producer not like someone collecting pretty backgrounds.

The Bottom Line

Locations do not just affect how your film looks. They affect how it sounds, how much it costs, how long it takes, and whether scenes are usable at all. A slightly less impressive location that runs smoothly will almost always beat a perfect-looking location that fights you at every step.

Choose locations that help you finish the film, not ones that create problems you did not budget for.

Clear Communication is Key

One of the biggest mistakes I see is filmmakers not being upfront with location owners about what a shoot really involves. Let me be clear, filming is messy. It does not matter whether it is a short scene or a major production. There will be people everywhere, equipment stacked in every corner, and a general sense of chaos.

Before you finalize a location, sit down with the owner and be brutally honest about what to expect. Let them know:

- There will be people coming and going, possibly for long hours.
- Equipment and cables will likely be set up throughout the space.
- It might not always be quiet, especially if you're filming dialogue or action scenes.

Make sure they understand the timeline, too. If you think you'll need the location from 2 PM to 5 PM, add extra hours on either side for setup, rehearsals, and cleanup. Trust me, shoots always run longer than expected. It's better to block out the whole day than to have someone tell you to pack up halfway through because they didn't know you'd be there so long.

The Golden Rule:

Leave it Better Than You Found It

This one is simple but crucial: leave the location exactly as you found it. If anything gets moved, whether it is furniture, décor, or even a vase, take photos before you start so you can put everything back in its place. This is normally the production designer's job, but they may not handle it properly if they are inexperienced.

I have heard horror stories of productions losing valuable items or damaging property. For example, a friend of mine rented a house for a feature film shoot. The owner was not properly briefed on what filming involved. After a few days of shooting, the place was a mess. The owner came by unexpectedly and saw it. Not understanding that everything would be put back exactly as it was once filming wrapped, he was furious and told them to pack up and leave. They had to continue shooting the film at another location and then try to match scenes. I cannot tell you what a nightmare that was for him. They ended up in a legal dispute that nearly tanked the project. Do not let that be you.

A few tips to keep things smooth:

• Assign a location manager (or take this on yourself if you're the producer). They'll be responsible for tracking what's moved, managing cleanup, and addressing any concerns.

• Budget for repairs or minor damages. Even with the best intentions, accidents happen. Equipment can scratch a wall, or a piece of furniture might get bumped. Have a contingency fund ready to handle these situations without stress. Get insurance if you can, especially if you are shooting in a place where there are expensive items of furniture, etc.

• If you're using a free location (lucky you!), treat it with even more care. A little goodwill can go a long way.

Get Everything in Writing

Before you roll a single camera, make sure you have a signed location release form. This document gives you the legal right to use the footage shot at that location.

Imagine this: you film for three days at a beautiful house, only for the owner to change their mind later and refuse to sign the release. Without that signature, you cannot legally use the footage. You would have to reshoot everything, and that could mean thousands of dollars down the drain.

So get the release signed before you start filming. No exceptions.

Expect the Unexpected

Even with all your planning, things can still go wrong. Neighbors might complain about the noise, or you might run into time constraints. I have been there, shooting in a small apartment complex late at night with 20 people crammed into a single unit. No matter how quiet we tried to be, the noise traveled. The neighbors were furious, and we were at risk of being kicked out before we finished the scene.

Luckily, the owner was understanding and let us push through, but it was a close call. If they had asked us to leave, it would have meant reshooting everything, and that is expensive. This is why it is so important to build a good relationship with the location owner.

Be respectful, keep them informed, and thank them sincerely when the shoot is over.

Think Beyond Houses and Offices

When you're on a tight budget, don't be afraid to get creative with locations. Local governments often have spaces like old buildings, schools, or community centers that they're looking to rent out. These can be a goldmine for low-budget filmmakers. Reach out and see what's available.

Here are a few other ideas:

• Friends and family: Just make sure they understand the scope of what you're asking.

• Local businesses: A café, bookstore, or even a warehouse can make for unique settings. They can also use this as promotion and marketing if they can use their actual business name.

• Public spaces: Parks or streets can work, but check with your local film office about permits.

Final Thoughts

Locations are one of the trickiest parts of filmmaking, but with careful planning, clear communication, and a little creativity, you can avoid most of the common pitfalls. Remember to:

• Be transparent with location owners about what's involved.

• Get everything in writing, location release forms are non-negotiable.

• Budget for damages or unexpected costs.

• Always leave the space better than you found it.

Most importantly, stay flexible. Even with the best-laid plans, things can go sideways. But if you're prepared, you'll be able to handle whatever comes your way and keep your production on track.

CHAPTER 14

PRE-PRODUCTION

THIS IS WHERE YOU LAY THE FOUNDATIONS...DON'T RUSH!

Pre-production is the part of filmmaking that most people rush through because they are eager to start shooting. It does not feel creative. It does not feel exciting. And yet, this is the phase where most serious problems either get solved quietly or planted like landmines for later.

By the time you roll the cameras, the film should already be protected. Not creatively. That comes later. It should be protected legally, logistically, and practically. Pre-production is where you create the conditions that allow production to run smoothly and, just as importantly, allow the film to be sold once it is finished.

This is where films either become manageable or fragile.

One of the first things that needs to happen in pre-production is the contracts. Not later. Not once things have calmed down. At the very beginning. If something or someone appears in your film, there needs to be an agreement in place. That applies to actors, crew, extras, locations, vehicles, artwork, music, props, everything. If it is visible on screen or essential to production, it must be cleared.

This is one of those areas where people assume they will sort it out later. Later rarely comes. And when it does, it is usually too late.

If you are working outside an English-speaking country, this is also the moment to think about language. Distributors, especially international ones, will expect documentation in English. That does not mean you need expensive legal software or complex systems. A simple bilingual contract, with your native language on one side and English on the other, is often enough. The point is clarity. Anyone reviewing your paperwork should be able to understand exactly what was agreed upon.

Pre-production is really about protecting the future of the film. It is very easy to finish a movie and only then discover you cannot sell it because something is missing. A release was not signed. A piece of artwork was not cleared. A location agreement was vague. These issues do not announce themselves early. They show up at the end, when distributors start asking questions and lawyers begin reviewing the material.

At that point, fixing problems becomes expensive, stressful, and sometimes impossible.

This is also where Errors and Omissions insurance comes into the picture. You will hear people talk about E&O as if it is just another checkbox. It is not. If a distributor requires it, the insurance company will review your film and your paperwork in detail. They will not insure the film unless everything is clean. Every contract, every license, and every release must be in order.

You do not need E&O on every low-budget film, but the moment you are aiming for serious distribution in the U.S., it becomes a gatekeeper. Pre-production is the only phase where you can realistically prepare for it.

Another thing that needs to happen in pre-production is delegation. Many producers try to do everything themselves, especially on smaller films. That usually works right up until production starts. Once the set is moving, people come and go quickly. Extras leave. Locations change. Crew members wrap and disappear. If releases are not collected at the right moment, they often never get collected at all.

That is why responsibility has to be assigned early. Someone needs to be in charge of the paperwork. Someone needs to check that forms are signed, usually the line producer. This does not require a large team, but it does require clarity. If everyone assumes someone else is handling it, no one is.

Pre-production is also where negotiations should be finished, not started. On independent films, you will almost certainly be asking people to work for less than they normally would. That is not unusual. Problems arise when expectations are vague. If someone is working for reduced pay, deferred payment, profit participation, or simply for the experience, that must be discussed clearly and put in writing before shooting begins.

Good intentions do not survive stress. Clear agreements do.

This is especially true when it comes to favors. Free locations, borrowed equipment, and discounted services can be incredibly helpful. They can also become a problem if assumptions are made. If someone is lending you something, ask very simple questions upfront. Is it free? Is there a limit? Will there be a fee later? What happens if something breaks? These conversations can feel awkward, but they are far less awkward than receiving an unexpected invoice after your budget is gone.

Pre-production is where you slow down enough to ask these questions properly.

A lot of the work in this phase feels small and boring at the time. How long exactly have you had the location? What happens if you go into overtime? Who is responsible if something gets damaged? These details do not feel important until they suddenly are. When they matter, they matter a great deal.

That is why pre-production is not something to rush through. It is not a formality between development and shooting. It is the phase where you protect yourself, your collaborators, and the film itself.

You can have a great shoot and still end up with a film you cannot sell if pre-production was careless. You can also survive a difficult shoot if pre-production is solid. The difference is rarely talent. It is preparation.

The goal of pre-production is not perfection. It is preparedness. Once the cameras roll, most of the things that truly matter are already locked in.

CHAPTER 15

POST-PRODUCTION

WHY THIS MATERS MORE THEN YOU THINK

You have shot your film. Congratulations. You have probably poured your heart and soul into production, but now comes the phase where your vision truly takes shape: post-production. This part of filmmaking is often overlooked during planning, but it is just as important as every other step, if not more. It can either make or break your film.

Let's talk about what to expect, who you will need, and how to navigate this exciting and sometimes overwhelming stage.

Assembling Your Dream Team

Filmmaking is a team effort, and in post-production, you'll need a few key players to bring it all together:

• The Editor

Think of the editor as the glue that holds your story together. They take all the footage you've shot and carefully weave it into a narrative that flows.

• The Audio Team

Audio is 40% of your film let that sink in for a second. You'll need someone to clean up dialogue, create soundscapes, and mix everything into a seamless experience. If you can find one person who handles all aspects of audio post (dialogue editing, sound effects, and mixing), great! If not, you might be working with multiple specialists, especially for larger projects.

• The Composer

Music is the emotional backbone of your film. Whether you hire someone to compose an original score or license stock music, the right soundtrack will elevate your film to a whole new level.

• The Colorist

This is the person who gives your film that unique, cinematic look. From balancing skin tones to creating a moody atmosphere, the colorist is essential for setting the tone of your story visually.

Start Early: Don't Wait Until It's Over

One of the smartest things you can do is get post-production rolling while you're still filming. If your budget allows, have your editor review dailies those raw, unedited clips from each shooting day.

Why is this so important?

• You can catch issues early. Maybe a crucial shot is out of focus or missing altogether. If you know this while you're still on set, you can fix it immediately rather than scrambling later.

• It saves time. By the time you wrap filming, your editor might already have a rough assembly of the movie ready for you to review.

This is especially critical for low-budget productions. When resources are tight, you can't afford surprises at the end.

The Locked Edit: The Golden Rule

Here's one of the biggest lessons of post-production: you need a locked edit before moving forward.

What's a locked edit?

It's the final, "this-is-it" version of your film. No more cutting scenes, switching takes, or shuffling things around.

Why is this so important?

• For Audio: Your sound designer needs precise timecode to sync dialogue, sound effects, and music. If you make changes to the edit later, their work will no longer line up, and they'll have to redo almost everything.

• For Grading: Your colorist works frame by frame. If you change the edit after they've started, you're essentially asking them to redo a lot of their work.

Of course, emergencies happen, and changes might be unavoidable. But keep these to an absolute minimum. Your team and your budget will thank you.

Audio: The Secret Weapon of Great Films

You've probably heard this before, but it's worth repeating: bad sound can ruin a good film. Audiences might forgive less-than-perfect visuals, but if they can't hear what's going on or the sound feels off, they'll check out.

Here's what your audio specialist will focus on:

• Dialogue Cleanup: Removing background noise, balancing levels, and making sure every word is crisp and clear.

• Sound Design: Creating all the little (and not-so-little) sounds that bring your world to life, footsteps, doors creaking, wind blowing, you name it.

• Foley: All natural sounds that happen will have to be re-recorded and placed within the movie, so that they can be on a separate track.

• Mixing: Ensuring all the elements (dialogue, music, effects) work together harmoniously.

If your film relies heavily on sound like a horror movie with jump scares or a sci-fi film with complex soundscapes this step might take longer. But even for simpler projects, sound is where your film can truly shine.

Music: Scoring the Emotion

Music does more than fill the silence; it sets the emotional tone of your film. Think about your favorite movie moments. Chances are, the music played a huge role in making them memorable.

If you can afford a composer, amazing! They'll craft a score that's unique to your story. If not, don't worry there's a ton of high-quality stock music out there. The key is finding tracks that feel authentic to your film's mood.

Pro tip: Work closely with your composer or music supervisor to decide where music is most effective. Sometimes less is more, and silence can be just as powerful as a soaring score.

Grading: The Art of Visual Storytelling

This is where your film gets its visual "look." Color grading isn't just about making things look pretty; it's about storytelling. A good colorist can:

• Create Atmosphere: Think warm, golden hues for a nostalgic feel or cold, desaturated tones for a thriller.

• Enhance Mood: Darken shadows for suspense, brighten scenes for comedy the possibilities are endless.

• Ensure Consistency: Fix any mismatched lighting or colors between shots so your film feels seamless.

Grading is especially crucial for genre films where visuals play a big role in creating atmosphere. Plan for at least a week or two for this step, depending on the complexity of your film.

Timing and Budget: Plan Wisely

Post-production takes time. How much? It depends on your project, but here's a rough guide:

• Editing: A few weeks to months, depending on how quickly you can lock your edit.

• Audio: 1–2 months, longer if your film has a lot of sound design.

• Grading: 1–2 weeks, but it could take longer for effects-heavy projects.

Make sure you've saved enough money for post-production. It's heartbreaking to see filmmakers run out of funds at this stage, leaving their films unfinished or poorly polished.

Stay Involved, but Don't Micromanage

The director will naturally want to oversee every step of the process, and he or she should. But make sure they remember that you hired professionals for a reason. They should trust their expertise and let them take the reins when needed.

Final Thoughts: The Magic of Post-Production

Post-production is where the raw materials of your film are shaped into the final masterpiece. It's exciting, it's challenging, and it's where all your hard work pays off.

To recap:

• Build your team early editor, audio, composer, and colorist.

• Start editing during production to catch issues early.

• Lock your edit before moving to sound and grading.

• Treat audio and music as essential storytelling tools.

• Plan your time and budget carefully.

Approach this phase with care, patience, and collaboration, and you'll end up with a film that's as polished and professional as anything on the big screen. You've got this!

CHAPTER 16

BILLING BLOCKS AND CREDITS

WHY THIS MATERS MORE THEN YOU THINK

Credits are one of those things nobody worries about until suddenly everyone cares.

Early on, people are usually relaxed. Everyone is excited. Everyone is focused on getting the film made. Credits feel like a future problem, something that can be figured out later.

That is a mistake.

Credits, billing blocks, and name placement are not just about recognition. They are about contracts, expectations, leverage, and, in some cases, legal disputes. If you do not address them properly during negotiations, they will come back at the worst possible moment, usually when the film is finished, sold, and money is involved.

Let's break this down in a way that actually makes sense.

What a Billing Block Actually Is

The billing block is the small block of text you see at the bottom of a poster, trailer, or other marketing materials. It lists the key credits: producers, director, writer, principal cast, production companies, and sometimes financiers.

This is not decorative text. It is contractual.

The order of names, the size of the text, and who is included or excluded are often specified in contracts, especially for actors, producers, and key creatives. Once a film is sold, distributors will ask for the billing block. If you do not have clear agreements in place, this is where disagreements begin.

And they can get very serious, very fast.

Front Credits vs End Credits

There is a significant difference between front credits and end credits, and that difference needs to be understood early.

Front credits appear at the beginning of the film. They are limited, highly visible, and often reserved for key crew and talent. End credits are longer, more inclusive, and traditionally where the all of the cast and crew are listed.

Who appears where is not random. It is usually negotiated.

Actors, directors, writers, and producers may have strong feelings or contractual requirements about whether they appear in the opening credits, the closing credits, or both. Once these expectations are set, changing them later can lead to conflict.

This is why credits should never be an afterthought. They should be discussed when contracts are signed, not when the edit is locked.

IMDb Credits Matter More Than You Think

IMDb may feel informal, but for many people in the industry, it functions as a professional résumé.

Credit placement on IMDb affects how people are perceived, how they are found in searches, and sometimes how future employers or collaborators evaluate them. Incorrect credits, missing credits, or mislabeled roles can cause real damage to professional relationships.

Who is credited as a producer?

Who is listed as executive producer versus associate producer?

Who controls the final credit list?

These are not trivial questions. They should be agreed upon in writing.

Posters and Marketing Materials Are Part of the Deal

Once a film is sold, posters, trailers, and marketing materials are created quickly. Distributors may ask for approvals, or they may proceed based on the information they have.

If contracts do not clearly specify billing, you may find yourself in disputes you did not anticipate. Actors may object to their name placement. Producers may argue over order. Financiers may expect visibility that was never agreed upon.

From the distributor's perspective, this is a problem they do not want. From your perspective, it can delay releases, damage relationships, and create legal exposure.

All of this can be avoided with clarity upfront.

Why Credits Become Legal Problems

Credits turn into legal issues when expectations are not aligned.

If someone believes they were promised a specific credit or a particular placement, and that promise is not honored, disputes can arise. These disputes often surface after the film is sold, when emotions are high and leverage shifts.

At that point, even small disagreements can escalate.

The safest approach is simple:

If it matters to someone, put it in the contract.

That does not mean everyone gets everything they want. It means everyone knows what they are agreeing to.

The Producer's Responsibility

As a producer, this is your responsibility.

You do not need to be an expert in media law, but you do need to understand that credits are not just vanity. They are currency. They affect careers. They shape future opportunities. And they influence how people feel about their involvement in your project.

Discuss credits during negotiations. Be clear about what you can and cannot offer. Make sure agreements are written down, included in contracts. Once agreed, honor them.

Nothing damages trust faster than changing credit arrangements after the fact.

The Bottom Line

Credits feel emotional because they are personal, but they must be handled professionally.

If you take one thing away from this chapter, let it be this:

If it is important enough to argue about later, it is important enough to agree on now.

Clear credit agreements protect you, protect your collaborators, and protect the film. They reduce disputes, prevent delays, and help ensure that when your film is finally out in the world, everyone feels fairly represented.

That is far easier to manage before the cameras roll than after the film is already sold.

CHAPTER 17

SALES AGENTS

Sales agents are some of the most important people you will work with if you are looking to sell your film. In many ways, they function like real estate agents, serving as the intermediary between you, the producer, and the distributor or buyer. Their role is vital because they have the network and industry knowledge that you, as an independent filmmaker, likely do not.

Why is their network so important? Selling a film is not just about having a strong product. It is about trust and relationships. The film industry operates on high stakes, and buyers prefer to work with people they know or trust to deliver quality projects. As a newcomer, breaking into that circle can be nearly impossible without support. Sales agents bridge that gap because they have access to a wide range of distributors, video-on-demand platforms, and other potential buyers.

How Sales Agents Work

When you work with a sales agent, you will typically agree to terms under which they represent your film for a specific period. They will then take a commission from every sale they make, usually between 15–25%, with 20% being the average.

In addition to commissions, some agents charge a marketing expense to cover the cost of promoting your film to potential buyers. This may include taking your film to markets, pitching it to distributors, and covering expenses such as travel or promotional materials. For example, a sales agent might charge $2,000 annually for marketing. While this can be reasonable in some cases, it can also become contentious because some agents misuse it by deducting excessive amounts without proper accountability.

Here's a simple breakdown:

- Suppose your film sells to a distributor for $10,000.
- The sales agent takes a 20% commission that's $2,000.
- They may also deduct a pre-agreed marketing fee of $1,000 from that $10,000.
- This means you receive $7,000 from the sale

Revenue Share Deals and Minimum Guarantees (MGs)

One of the most common ways sales agents and distributors work is through revenue share deals. Here's how it typically works:

• The distributor offers a Minimum Guarantee (MG) a lump sum payment for the rights to your film. For instance, they might pay $10,000 upfront.

• The distributor then resells or exploits your film (e.g., through theatrical releases, VOD, or licensing) to recoup their $10,000 investment.

• Once they've recouped their MG, any further revenue is split between you and the distributor. This split is often 70% (to you) and 30% (to the distributor), but it varies depending on the deal.

Here's the catch: between the distributor's 30% and the sales agent's 20%, you're essentially giving away 50% of every dollar earned from your film. And that's after the distributor has already recouped their MG.

This harsh reality highlights why it's so challenging to make a profit in the film industry, especially given the high cost of production. It's also why you should aim to produce your film as cost-effectively as possible. The smaller your budget, the better your chances of breaking even or turning a profit.

Do You Need a Sales Agent?

The short answer: not always. While sales agents can be incredibly helpful, they're not your only option. You can choose to sell your film directly to distributors, but doing so requires thorough knowledge of the film sales process.

If you go this route, you must:

1. Learn the details of film sales contracts, revenue splits, deliverables, and negotiation strategies.

2. Establish relationships with distributors and build trust over time.

3. Avoid mistakes that could sour your reputation. If you mishandle a deal or fail to deliver on expectations, distributors might refuse to work with you again, and in a tight-knit industry, word travels fast.

Plan for Sales

One of the smartest moves you can make is planning for sales before you even start production. While it's not always possible, pre-selling your film can alleviate a lot of financial stress. If you can lock in distribution deals early, you'll have a clearer idea of your budget and revenue potential.

Final Thoughts on Sales Agents

Sales agents are powerful allies in the world of film distribution, but they're not the only path forward. Whether you work with an agent or go it alone, the key is to approach the process with knowledge and preparation. Research your options, build relationships, and always plan for how you'll sell your film long before it's finished.

Remember, the film industry is built on trust and connections. Respect those relationships, and you'll have a better shot at long-term success.

CHAPTER 18

DISTRIBUTORS

L et's talk about distributors, your key partners in getting your film into the world. Distributors are the lifeblood of your film's journey to its audience. They buy the rights to your film in one form or another and are responsible for ensuring your project reaches cinemas, television, streaming platforms, airlines, or wherever else it fits. In practical terms, these are the people you are creating for, because if they do not want your film, it will be difficult to get it seen.

This is why it is crucial to ensure distributors are genuinely interested in your film. If it does not resonate with them or if it falls outside the genres they focus on, you may find yourself with a project that no one is willing to acquire. Building relationships with distributors and targeting the right ones is essential. Do not approach a distributor known for romantic comedies with your horror film. Instead, do your research and focus on distributors who specialize in your film's genre.

What Do Distributors Actually Do?

As the name implies, distributors distribute your film. They use their networks and expertise to sell it to their clients, such as cinemas, streaming platforms such as Netflix or Tubi, television networks, airlines, and others. Their goal is to place your film where it has the best chance of being seen while maximizing their profits.

Distributors operate on a territorial basis. For example, a U.S. distributor might acquire the rights to your film for North America, meaning the United States and Canada, typically for a set period of time, such as ten years. Once they acquire those rights, they will sell your film to various platforms within that territory. For example, they might license it to Tubi, a U.S.-based advertising-supported video-on-demand platform, and you could receive either a revenue share or a minimum guarantee upfront.

The Challenges of Working with Distributors

While distributors are vital, working with them isn't always smooth sailing. Some distributors have a reputation for not being entirely transparent. For example:

• They might sell your film to multiple platforms or territories without informing you once the MG has been recouped.

• They may delay payments or fail to provide clear documentation of sales and revenue.

Because of this, it's critical to keep a close eye on your film's sales and revenue. Request regular reports and make sure the terms in your contract are clear about transparency and payment schedules.

Another challenge is the marketing expenses distributors charge. Just like sales agents, distributors may deduct costs for promoting your film, attending markets, or creating marketing materials. Always ensure these expenses are reasonable and capped at, say $10,000 so you're not blindsided by excessive deductions.

Maximizing Your Film's Potential with Distributors

Selling your film to distributors isn't a quick or easy process. It takes time, effort, and a lot of conversations. Here are some tips to help you navigate this process:

1. Sell to as many territories as possible.

Don't just focus on one country. For instance, South Korean distributors often purchase European and American films, so they could be a great market for your project. Similarly, explore opportunities in countries like Australia, Thailand, and others.

2. Build relationships with local distributors.

Distributors often specialize in their own territories, so look for partners in each region who understand their market and audience.

3. Focus on the MG.

The MG is guaranteed money in your pocket, so try to negotiate the highest MG possible upfront. This provides a financial safety net as you wait for additional revenue to come in.

4. Communicate with your sales agent.

If you're working with a sales agent, it's crucial to coordinate with them. Let them know if you're planning to approach a distributor directly. Nothing sours relationships faster than overlapping efforts if you and your sales agent both pitch to the same distributor, it can damage the agent's relationship (and your reputation). Always check with them first to avoid missteps.

5. Stay organized and vigilant.

Keep track of all agreements, sales, and payments. Ask distributors for detailed documentation on where your film is sold, how much revenue it's generating, and any deductions they're making.

Is It Worth Selling Directly to Distributors?

If you're the producer and you're handling the sales yourself without a sales agent it's definitely possible to approach distributors directly. However, it requires a lot of work and attention to detail. If you choose this route, you'll need to:

- Research which distributors are a good fit for your film.
- Reach out to them with a solid pitch.
- Negotiate contracts carefully to ensure you're protected.

If you are also working with a sales agent, make sure you negotiate a clause that allows you to retain 100% of any deals you secure independently. Some agents will agree to this, while others may still claim a commission on all sales, regardless of how they are made.

You will essentially be cold calling, so be prepared for rejection. These people are incredibly busy.

What is even more important, if you are pursuing sales alongside your sales agent, is that you keep them informed about exactly who you are contacting. If you overlap, it can create significant problems for both of you.

Final Thoughts on Distributors

Distributors are your allies, but navigating the relationship can be complex. The key is to stay informed, communicate openly, and protect yourself with clear contracts and documentation. Be prepared for a long process. It often takes time to see meaningful returns, especially if you are selling to multiple territories.

By staying organized, targeting the right markets, and building strong relationships, you can maximize your film's potential and give it the best chance of reaching audiences worldwide. It is hard work, but it is absolutely possible. Stay determined.

CHAPTER 19

UNDERSTANDING BUYOUT CONTRACTS

When a distributor or buyer wants to acquire your film, you will receive a contract. For most independent filmmakers, that document will be a buyout agreement — sometimes called a Negative Pickup Agreement or an Acquisition Agreement. It will be long, dense, and written in legal language designed more for lawyers than filmmakers. But understanding what is in it, what you are agreeing to, and what the implications are is not optional. It is one of the most important things you will do for your film and your career.

This chapter walks you through the core sections of a buyout contract in plain language. The goal is not to make you a lawyer — it is to make you an informed filmmaker who knows what questions to ask, what to watch out for, and when to push back. Before signing any contract, always engage a qualified entertainment attorney to review it on your behalf.

What Is a Buyout?

A buyout is exactly what it sounds like: the buyer pays you a fixed sum and in return acquires broad, long-term rights to your film. Unlike a licensing deal — where you retain ownership and lease rights for a defined period or territory — a buyout typically transfers sweeping rights to the buyer, often permanently and across the entire world.

The word buyout tells you something important about the structure. The buyer is buying their way out of ongoing financial obligations. Instead of paying you a percentage of revenue every time the film earns money, they pay an agreed amount upfront (or in installments) and acquire the rights to exploit the film as they see fit. For you, this means certainty about what you will receive. But it also means relinquishing control, and giving up any share of future upside if the film performs well.

The Parties, the Date, and the Definitions

Every contract opens by identifying who is involved — the buyer and you (or your production company) — and dating the agreement. That date matters because it starts the clock on every deadline that follows: delivery windows, payment schedules, and notice periods all typically run from the date of full execution, meaning when all parties have signed.

Immediately after the opening, most contracts include a definitions section. This is where the real scope of the deal is established, and it is where many filmmakers stop paying close enough attention. Four definitions in particular shape the entire agreement.

The Territory defines where the buyer can exploit the film. "The Universe" or "Worldwide" means everywhere, without limitation. A more restricted territory might be a single country or region. The Term defines how long the rights last. "In perpetuity" means forever — there is no expiry date, and the rights will never return to you automatically. The Rights define what the buyer can actually do with the film, and in a typical buyout this list is extensive: theatrical, television, streaming, home video, digital download, merchandising, music publishing, sequels, remakes, podcasts, radio, theme parks, and more. And Delivery defines what you must hand over and by when, which links to a detailed schedule we will cover shortly.

Read every definition carefully. A contract with a universal territory, a perpetual term, and a broad rights definition is the most expansive deal possible. Make sure the financial terms reflect that.

The Grant of Rights

The grant of rights section is the heart of the agreement. It is where you formally transfer ownership of the film — and usually its underlying material, including the screenplay and all characters — to the buyer. In a full buyout, this transfer is irrevocable. Once you have signed, you cannot take it back.

Beyond the core transfer, this section typically grants the buyer the right to edit, modify, adapt, and change the film in any way they choose — including altering the title, cutting scenes, changing the ending, adding dubbing, or creating sequel stories based on your characters. The buyer acts in their sole discretion, meaning they do not need to consult you.

Most buyout contracts also include a moral rights waiver. Moral rights — known in French law as droit moral — are a creator's rights to attribution and to object to changes that damage their reputation. By waiving them, you agree not to take legal action even if the buyer makes changes to your film that you believe are artistically harmful. This waiver applies globally and is typically irrevocable.

Many agreements also classify all production services as work made for hire, a legal doctrine under which the buyer, not you, is treated as the legal author of the work for copyright purposes. The practical effect is that copyright vests in the buyer from the outset.

Understanding the full scope of what you are giving up in this section is essential. It is not simply the right to screen the film. It is the right to remake it, sequel it, merchandise it, adapt it, alter it, and exploit it in any medium that currently exists or may exist in the future.

The Purchase Price and Payment Schedule

The total purchase price in a buyout is rarely paid in a single lump sum. Almost universally, it is structured as a series of installments, each tied to a specific milestone: a portion on signing, another portion within thirty days of execution, another on accepted delivery, another on initial commercial release, and further amounts at intervals after release — six months and eighteen months are common.

This structure has significant implications. The full amount you are owed may take two years or more to arrive, and several of the later payments are contingent on things the buyer controls — most importantly, the decision to commercially release the film. If the contract does not obligate the buyer to release the film within a defined period, there is a risk that those later installments never come due. Push to include a release obligation with a specific deadline, and if possible, negotiate a reversion clause: a provision that returns the rights to you if the buyer fails to release the film or misses a payment.

Delivery

Delivery is one of the most demanding and most underestimated obligations in a buyout deal. It is not simply handing over a digital file of the film. A full delivery package typically includes the finished film master in a specific technical format (codec, resolution, color space, frame rate, audio configuration), a stereo and surround sound mix, an M&E track — that is, a music and effects track with no dialogue, used for dubbing into other languages — subtitle and caption files, a finished trailer, and textless versions of any shots containing graphics.

On the legal side, delivery usually requires chain of title documentation proving your ownership of all rights, a music cue sheet listing every piece of music in the film with clearance confirmation, signed music synchronization and master use licenses, cast and crew agreements, copyright registrations, a copyright search, a title search, a certificate of origin, and often an Errors and Omissions insurance policy — a specialist insurance product that protects against claims of copyright infringement or defamation.

Marketing deliverables are also typically required: layered Photoshop key artwork files in specified dimensions, a minimum number of high-resolution production stills, a metadata file containing synopsis, cast list, chapter points, and rating information.

Delivery is not deemed complete until the buyer has reviewed and accepted everything. A single missing document or a file that does not meet technical specifications can delay acceptance, and with it, your payment. The contract will almost certainly state that time is of the essence for delivery, meaning a missed deadline is a material breach. The practical advice is simple: treat the delivery requirements as a production checklist from day one, not as something to worry about when the film is finished.

Representations, Warranties, and Indemnification

In signing a buyout contract, you make a series of legal promises to the buyer about the film. These are called representations and warranties, and they typically include: that you own all rights being transferred, that the film does not infringe any third-party intellectual property, that all music has been cleared for all media in perpetuity, that you have obtained all necessary releases from cast, crew, and locations, that there are no debts or liens attached to the film, and that the film has not been previously licensed in any way that conflicts with this agreement.

These are not formalities. If any of them turns out to be untrue — even if you genuinely did not know — you may be in breach and liable for the buyer's losses. The indemnification clause, which typically follows, reinforces this: if a third party sues the buyer because of something you warranted to be clear, you may be required to cover the buyer's legal costs and any damages awarded.

Two practical points here. First, do not make any representation you cannot verify. Do not warrant that all music is cleared unless you have the signed licenses in your hands. Do not warrant that all talent releases are in place unless you have reviewed every agreement. Second, obtain Errors and Omissions insurance before delivery. It is specifically designed to cover these risks, and most buyers require it.

Credits, Guilds, and Governing Law

Credits in film are often contractual obligations, not just courtesies. Your agreements with the director, writer, and principal cast may impose specific requirements about how their names appear, in what size, and in what position — both on screen and in paid advertising. A buyout contract will require you to deliver a complete credit statement listing every obligation. Discrepancies between what you have promised people and what appears in the film can create costly disputes down the line.

If your film was produced under a guild or union agreement — with the Directors Guild, the Writers Guild, or SAG-AFTRA, for example — you must disclose this. Guild status carries obligations around credits, residuals, and working conditions that transfer with the rights. Misrepresenting guild status is a serious problem.

Finally, the governing law and dispute resolution clause establishes which country's or state's laws apply and where any legal dispute would be resolved — in court or through arbitration. If you are based in one country and the buyer is in another, this clause determines where you would have to pursue your rights if something goes wrong. Negotiating for a jurisdiction that is accessible to you, or for international arbitration as a neutral mechanism, is worth doing.

Before You Sign

Every filmmaker who receives a buyout contract should do the same things before signing. Engage an entertainment attorney — not a general solicitor or a family friend who happens to be a lawyer, but someone who works in entertainment law and understands the industry. Read the definitions carefully, particularly Territory, Term, Rights, and Delivery. Audit your delivery package against the schedule in the contract and confirm you can actually meet it. Verify that every piece of music in the film is properly cleared for the scope of rights being granted. Have an attorney review your chain of title. And take the time you need — a legitimate buyer will not pressure you to sign immediately.

A buyout contract transfers significant value and control. Understanding what you are agreeing to is not just good legal practice. It is the difference between a deal that works for you and one that simply works against you.

For a detailed section-by-section guide to buyout contracts — including a full breakdown of delivery requirements, music clearance obligations, the implications of moral rights waivers, and a pre-signing checklist — download the extended reference guide available at https://zoltanlaszlodeak.kit.com/fe6378626b

CHAPTER 20

DELIVERY REQUIREMENTS

Delivery requirements are one of the biggest shocks for first-time filmmakers.

You spend years developing, financing, shooting, and editing a film. You finally secure a deal. You think you are done. Then the distributor sends you a document titled something like "Delivery Requirements," and suddenly it feels like a foreign language.

This chapter exists to make sure that does not happen to you. I am not going to turn you into a technician. That is not the goal. What you do need is a clear understanding of what distributors are asking for, why they ask for it, and who typically prepares these materials. While your editor or colorist will handle most of the technical work, you are responsible for ensuring everything exists and is delivered correctly.

The Feature Video File (Your Actual Movie)

This is the master version of your film, the highest-quality version that will ever exist. Distributors do not want an MP4, a Vimeo link, or a compressed file. They want a large, uncompressed, professional master that can be used for streaming platforms, broadcast, and future formats.

Think of this as the film's negative. Everything else will be created from this file.

This is almost always exported by your editor or post-production house, sometimes with input from the colorist and sound mixer. Your job as a producer is not to create it, but to ensure it exists in the correct format and has not been compromised by shortcuts earlier in post-production.

Audio: Dialogue, Music, and Effects Separated

Distributors do not just want the finished sound mix. They also require the music and sound effects to be separated from the dialogue. Why? Because your film may be dubbed into other languages. When that happens, the dialogue is replaced, but the music and effects remain.

This is why you will hear the term M&E, meaning Music and Effects. It is a version of the soundtrack with no dialogue. This is handled by your sound designer or re-recording mixer, not by you. However, you need to know it is coming. If you did not plan for this during sound post-production, creating it later can be expensive or even impossible.

Subtitles and Closed Captions

Subtitles are for translation. Closed captions are for accessibility. Distributors may require subtitles if your film includes dialogue in multiple languages, and they may require closed captions if they already exist or are mandated by certain platforms. The important thing to understand is that subtitles and captions are separate files, not burned into the image. You cannot simply hard-code them into the picture and consider the job done. These files are usually created by a specialist service, sometimes through your distributor and sometimes independently. Your role is to budget for them and ensure they are accurate. Poor subtitles can make a film look amateurish very quickly.

Textless Elements (Removing On-Screen Words)

Any time your film includes text on screen, such as opening titles, lower thirds, location names, or end credits, distributors may ask for a version of those shots without the text. This allows them to replace English text with another language later. These are called textless elements, and they are often forgotten until the last minute. They are created by your editor or post-production house, but only if the original project files still exist and are properly organized. If you flatten everything too early, recreating textless versions can be difficult and time-consuming.

Trailer Deliverables

If your contract includes a trailer, it comes with its own delivery requirements. Just like the feature, distributors often require a high-quality master file of the trailer, along with separate music and effects tracks, subtitles, captions, and sometimes textless elements. The trailer may feel like marketing, but from a delivery perspective, it is treated very seriously. It must meet the same technical and legal standards as the feature.

Legal Deliverables (This Is Where Producers Live)

This is the part most producers underestimate.

Legal deliverables are not files you export from editing software. They are documents that prove you own the film and have the right to sell it.

This includes contracts with writers, directors, actors, composers, and producers. It includes proof that music is properly licensed. It includes copyright registrations, title searches, and formal credit statements.

This is where your earlier chapters on contracts, credits, and paperwork come together. If something is missing at this stage, a distributor can delay payment or walk away entirely.

Billing Blocks and Credit Statements

Distributors will ask for a detailed breakdown of who is credited, how they are credited, and where their credit appears.

This includes on-screen credits, poster credits, and paid advertising credits. They want to see what was contractually promised and whether it has been delivered correctly.

This is why credits must be negotiated early and put in writing. Delivery is where those promises are verified.

Music Cue Sheets

A cue sheet is a document that lists every piece of music in your film, where it appears, how long it plays, and who owns it.

This is not optional. It is required so royalties can be tracked and paid properly.

Cue sheets are often created by the composer, music supervisor, or post-production team, but the producer is responsible for delivering them.

Marketing Materials

Distributors also need assets to sell your film.

This includes poster artwork, still photographs, metadata, and exhibition history. These materials help platforms describe, categorize, and promote your film.

If you did not take proper stills during production, this is where you will regret it. Screen grabs are not a replacement for professional promotional photography.

A Very Important Reality Check

Most of the technical deliverables are prepared by professionals: editors, colourists, sound mixers, and post-production houses.

Your job is not to press the buttons.

Your job is to:

- know what will be required
- plan for it early
- budget for it
- and make sure nothing is missing

Delivery requirements are not punishment. They are how the industry protects itself.

Once you understand that, they become manageable.

The Big Picture

A film is not finished when it is edited.

A film is finished when it is delivered.

Understanding delivery requirements early allows you to make smarter decisions during production and post-production. Ignoring them means scrambling at the end, spending money you did not plan for, and risking deals that took years to secure.

This chapter is not here to scare you.

It is here to make sure you are not surprised.

Because in filmmaking, surprises are almost always expensive.

CHAPTER 21

IN CONCLUSION

I want to wrap this up by saying that everything I have shared in this book is based on my personal experiences, the things I went through, the people I met, the people I worked with, and, of course, the films I made. It felt important to put all of this into a book because I believe it can make a real difference for someone about to embark on the incredible and challenging journey of making their first feature film.

I hope that by reading this, you step into your project better informed and more prepared, so you can avoid some of the mistakes I made. I wanted to take those missteps and hard lessons I learned the difficult way and turn them into something that could help someone else. As I have said from the very beginning, the variety of roles I have held in my career, working across departments, serving as a sales agent, working in television, and in other industries, has given me a broad perspective. I hope that perspective has been valuable to you as a reader and has offered insights you might not have gained elsewhere. There may be ideas I have repeated. That was intentional, to reinforce their importance.

If you have made it to the end of this book, thank you for taking the time to read it. I genuinely hope you have found it useful. I did not intend this to be an exhaustive guide that dives deeply into every subject. There are already books with hundreds of pages dedicated to a single aspect of filmmaking. Instead, my goal was to give you a broad, practical view of the filmmaking and distribution process.

I wrote this with the assumption that most readers, people like you, already have some experience in filmmaking. You are likely already part of the industry, or at least connected to others who are. My goal was to give you a guide to understand the bigger picture: what you need to research, the paths you might take, and the people you will need to work with, whether that is a sales agent, a distributor, or another key collaborator who can help you make, sell, or distribute your film.

To anyone who has finished this book and is ready to dive into a first feature film, I wish you nothing but success. If you would like to reach out, my contact details are included at the end of this book. While I cannot promise that I will be able to respond to everyone, I would genuinely love to hear from you, especially if you have made your film and found any part of this book helpful. Knowing that something I have shared has contributed, even in a small way, to your success would make the effort of writing this book worthwhile.

Thank you again for reading. Take care, and best of luck with all your future filmmaking endeavors.

Please leave a review on whichever platform you bought my book, it will help others decide if they will want to read it and help me improve on my writing in the future. Thank you.

BONUS CONTENT

The materials here are the practical stuff — the kind of content that becomes essential once your project starts moving toward financing and production. It didn't fit naturally into the flow of the main book, but it's some of the most requested material from filmmakers who are actively developing their first film.

Scan the QR code and you'll get access to an extended contract reference guide, a full breakdown of buyout agreements, delivery checklists, and a pre-signing checklist you can use every time an acquisition offer lands on your desk. You'll also find interviews with working sales agents, distributors, and independent producers sharing what they've learned from the inside — the candid, practical stuff that rarely makes it into any classroom.

Once you're signed up, you'll be kept in the loop on webinars, one-on-one mentorship opportunities, and other content as it comes. Think of it as a resource that grows with you, not just something you read once and shelve.

https://zoltanlaszlodeak.kit.com/fe6378626b

Scan to sign up.

The Author

Zoltan L Deak

Zoltan is a filmmaker, producer, and entrepreneur who has successfully taken a feature film from concept to sale. With experience spanning production, sales, and marketing, he shares practical, nononsense insights to help emerging filmmakers navigate the realities of the industry.